CONTENTS

(R)   *indicates Rhythmic Reading exercises*

MUSIC
FOR
SIGHT SINGING

Ninth Edition

NANCY ROGERS
College of Music
Florida State University

ROBERT W. OTTMAN
Emeritus
College of Music
University of North Texas

PEARSON

Boston Columbus Indianapolis New York San Francisco Upper Saddle River
Amsterdam Cape Town Dubai London Madrid Milan Munich Paris Montreal Toronto
Delhi Mexico City São Paulo Sydney Hong Kong Seoul Singapore Taipei Tokyo

Editor-in-Chief: Sarah Touborg
Editorial Director: Craig Campanella
Senior Publisher: Roth Wilkofsky
Director of Marketing: Brandy Dawson
Executive Marketing Manager: Kate Mitchell
Marketing Assistant: Paige Patunas
Senior Managing Editor: Melissa Feimer
Production Liaison: Joe Scordato
Full-Service Management: S4Carlisle Publishing Services
Production Editor: Sudha Balasundaram/S4Carlisle
Photo Research and Permissions: Ben Ferrini
Senior Operations Specialist: Diane Peirano
Manufacturing and Operations Manager: Mary Fischer
Cover Image: Fotolia © Pink Badger
Cover Designer: Bruce Kenselaar
Creative Director (Cover): Jayne Conte
Senior Digital Media Editor: David Alick
Digital Media Project Manager: Rich Barnes
Composition: S4Carlisle Publishing Services
Printer/Binder: LSC Communications/Crawfordsville
Cover Printer: Lehigh-Phoenix Color/Hagerstown

Credits and acknowledgments borrowed from other sources and reproduced, with permission, in this textbook appear on appropriate page within text or on pages xix–xx.

Library of Congress Cataloging-in-Publication Data

Ottman, Robert W.
  Music for sight singing/ Nancy Rogers, Robert W. Ottman.—9th ed.
    p. cm.
  Some selections contain words.
  ISBN-13: 978-0-205-93833-9
  ISBN-10: 0-205-93833-7
  1. Sight-singing. I. Rogers, Nancy. II. Title.
  MT870.O86 2013
  781.4′23–dc23

                                                  2012030180

10   17

Student Edition:
ISBN-10: 0-205-93833-7
ISBN-13: 978-0-205-93833-9
Instructor's Resource Copy:
ISBN-10: 0-205-93968-6
ISBN-13: 978-0-205-93968-8

PART II
MELODY: DIATONIC INTERVALS
RHYTHM: SUBDIVISION OF THE BEAT

PART III
MELODY: CHROMATICISM
RHYTHM: FURTHER RHYTHMIC PRACTICES

PREFACE

Developing the "mind's ear"—the ability to imagine how music sounds without first playing it on an instrument—is essential to any musician, and sight singing (in conjunction with ear training and other studies in musicianship) is invaluable in reaching this fundamental goal. The principal objective of sight singing is acquiring the ability to sing a given melody accurately at *first sight*. Although repeating a melody and correcting any errors is beneficial, we can truly sight sing a melody only once, which is why *Music for Sight Singing* provides a generous number of exercises (more than 1,400 in this volume) for practice.

Generations of musicians have valued *Music for Sight Singing* for its abundance of meticulously organized melodies drawn from the literature of composed music and a wide range of the world's folk music. Not only is "real music" more enjoyable and interesting to sing than dry exercises, but genuine repertoire naturally introduces a host of important musical considerations beyond pitch and rhythm (including dynamics, accents, articulations, slurs, repeat signs, and tempo markings). The book's systematic arrangement of exercises according to specific melodic and rhythmic features lays an effective foundation for success. Each chapter methodically introduces elements one at a time, steadily increasing in difficulty while providing a musically meaningful framework around which students can hone their skills. Through this method, the book creates a sense of challenge rather than frustration: a conscientious student should always be prepared to tackle the next melody.

The text as a whole is divided into four parts:

1. Chapters 1–9, diatonic melodies with rhythmic patterns limited to whole beats and their most basic divisions (two notes per beat in simple meters, three notes per beat in compound meters)
2. Chapters 10–12, diatonic melodies with rhythmic patterns that include subdivisions of the beat (four notes per beat in simple meters, six notes per beat in compound meters)

3. Chapters 13–19, chromaticism, tonicization, modulation, and more advanced rhythmic patterns and metrical concepts
4. Chapters 20–21, modal and post-tonal music

Music for Sight Singing contains exercises appropriate for students of all skill levels, including beginners, but a basic working knowledge of fundamental music theory and notation is prerequisite to sight singing. The following abilities are particularly important:

- Recognize, write, and sing all major and minor scales
- Recognize and write all major and minor key signatures
- Recognize and write all common note values and their corresponding rests
- Recognize and interpret standard meter signatures

Each of the above will be reviewed as topics are introduced throughout the text. However, a practical command of these basic elements from the outset will ensure satisfactory progress.

A new edition of *Music for Sight Singing* offers the opportunity to build on the book's strengths, address any weaknesses, and introduce some new ideas. As always, exercises have been selected from a wide musical repertoire, and melodies written especially for pedagogical purposes are kept to a minimum. Important revisions in the ninth edition include the following:

- Triplets in simple meters and duplets in compound meters are introduced much earlier, before chromaticism. Although the chapter that focuses specifically on these topics is shorter than it was in recent editions, triplets and duplets are used throughout the later chapters. The overall number of exercises containing triplets and duplets has not been reduced.
- Syncopation is also introduced earlier, before chromaticism. Again, readers familiar with previous editions will observe that the focal chapter is shorter, but the overall number of syncopated exercises remains the same.
- Chromaticism is introduced more gradually, starting with chromatic embellishing tones in the context of stepwise motion. The strong focus on tonicizing V before proceeding to a wide variety of other tonicizations remains.
- Modulation is also introduced more gradually, with a new section addressing modulation from a minor key to its relative major. The section focusing on modulation to the dominant now includes both major and minor keys.
- The number of melodies in minor keys has significantly increased.
- Many more melodies have been notated in bass clef.

The ninth edition of *Music for Sight Singing* will be well supported by MySearchLab, a collection of practical online materials and resources. MySearchLab improves teaching by enabling instructors to spend less class time checking homework and more class time addressing true sight singing, group activities, and listening skills. Through MySearchLab, students can conveniently submit their sight-singing performances online and receive detailed individual comments, but without sacrificing valuable class time; furthermore, they can review their own performances as well as the corresponding feedback at any time. Instructors can quickly and easily post assignments and additional material, and they can use online sight singing in the manner they prefer: for graded homework assignments that don't reduce productive class time, as a way to monitor student progress and/or practice time, or simply for providing extra assistance to students whose schedules preclude regular office hour visits. Practical features such as the online grade book and customizable grading rubrics help to keep class records accurate and organized.

Perhaps the most exciting component of MySearchLab is the Rhythm Generator, software developed primarily by William Wieland to create virtually unlimited rhythmic drills tailored to specific chapters of the book. These rhythmic drills are easily set to a variety of lengths as well as to beginning, intermediate, or advanced levels; they provide appropriate challenge to any student. Rhythm Generator exercises are not only ideal for in-class sight reading and for individual practice, but they can be used as an inexhaustible source for rhythm-reading exams. Instructors and students alike will find the rhythms well targeted, musically satisfying, and fun to perform.

As always, more melodies have been added than deleted in this edition, but (with the exception of copyrighted material from the last chapter) all of the deleted melodies remain available on MySearchLab. This edition maintains the significantly enlarged rhythm chapters and the structured improvisation exercises established in the seventh edition. Structured improvisation provides students with a framework around which to create their own melodies. These singing exercises are crafted to reinforce the lessons of their respective chapters, fundamentally emphasizing the book's organization and approach through a new kind of activity. Structured improvisation training offers specific musical and pedagogical benefits, from helping beginning students master an unfamiliar solmization system (by concentrating specifically on scale degrees and their corresponding syllables without the additional mental burden of notation) to fostering a deep awareness of harmony in students at all levels. Finally, improvisational exercises will provide additional variety to class and individual practice, and (unlike traditional sight singing) they will extend the same benefits even after multiple repetitions.

I am strongly committed to maintaining the tradition of excellence that Robert Ottman established more than 50 years ago. The combination of his vast knowledge of the repertoire and his deep pedagogical instincts made *Music for Sight Singing* one of the most celebrated music textbooks of the twentieth century. It is humbling to walk in such giant footsteps, but of course it is also a tremendous privilege to continue Dr. Ottman's work for the benefit of twenty-first-century musicians.

Nancy Rogers

IN MEMORIAM

Musicians around the world have been touched by Robert Ottman. Hundreds of fortunate students studied with him during his long career at the University of North Texas, where he is fondly remembered as an exceptionally fine and dedicated teacher. He was an inspirational role model for those who later became educators and were able to pass along his words of wisdom, his teaching techniques, and his high standards to thousands of their own students. Countless other musicians have benefited from the insight and experience that he poured into *Music for Sight Singing* and 10 other textbooks.

Dr. Ottman earned his bachelor's and master's degrees from the Eastman School of Music (1938 and 1944), then enlisted in the U.S. Army as a chaplain's assistant. During World War II, he played a portable organ during worship services and drove the chaplain's Jeep (sometimes at night, without headlights) near enemy territory in order to draw fire and pinpoint troop locations. After the war ended, he studied at Trinity College of Music in London, then returned to the United States to head the music theory department at the University of North Texas (known at the time as the North Texas State College). He received his doctorate from UNT in 1956—the same year that he published the first edition of *Music for Sight Singing*.

Serving both as a professor of music theory and as director of the Madrigal Singers, Robert Ottman was a valued member of the University of North Texas faculty throughout his 35 years there. Even after his retirement in 1981, he remained actively involved with the university and the larger Denton community. In 2004 he received the UNT President's Citation for outstanding service.

Dr. Ottman was beloved by those who knew him and, remarkably, even by people acquainted solely with his books. If it is, indeed, possible to be immortalized through one's work, then Robert Ottman will live forever in the hearts and minds of musicians all around the world.

Robert William Ottman
May 3, 1914–June 30, 2005

ACKNOWLEDGMENTS

The following publishers have granted permission to use melodies from their publications, for which the authors wish to express their appreciation. Additional acknowledgments will be found immediately below individual melodies.

American Book Company, New York: melody 2.29 from *Songs and Pictures,* Book I, by Robert Foresman.

The American Folklore Society, Philadelphia, PA: melodies 6.47, 12.24, 15.14 and 17.73 from *Spanish-American Folk Songs,* ed. Eleanor Hague; melodies 3.35 and 20.8 from *The Journal of American Folk Lore.*

Ascherberg, Hopwood, and Crew, Ltd.: melody 4.30 from *Folk Songs of the North-Countries* by Frank Kidson; melody 8.43 from *A Garland of English Folk Songs* by Frank Kidson.

Associated Music Publishers, Inc., New York, NY: melodies 17.30 and 17.56 from *Folk Dance Music of the Slavic Nations* by H. A. Schimmerling; melodies 3.9, 3.14, 3.16, 3.28, 5.26, and 17.67 from *Das Lied der Volker* by Heinrich Möller, copyright by B. Schott's Soehne, Mainz, used by permission of the copyright owner and its agent, Associated Music Publishers, Inc.

C.F. Peters Corporation, New York, NY: melodies 3.3, 3.61, 6.17, 6.39, and 8.26 from *Deutschland in Volkslied,* ed. Gustav Kniep, copyright C. F. Peters, reprinted with permission.

Columbia University Press, New York, NY: melody 4.74 from *A Song Catcher in the Southern Mountains* by Dorothy Scarborough; melodies 3.31, 3.50, 3.63, 12.41, 14.42, 14.61, 17.52 and 17.77 from *Folk Music and Poetry of Spain and Portugal* by Kurt Schindler, courtesy of Hispanic Institute, Columbia University.

G. Schirmer, Inc., New York, NY: melody 13.78 from *Anthology of Ialian Song* by A. Parisotti; melodies 6.48 and 15.1 from *44 French Songs and Variants* by Julian Tiersot; melody 6.25 from *Reliquary of English Song;* melody 4.87 from *Songs of Italy* by E. Marzo.

Gesellschaft zur Herausgabe von Denkmäler der Tonkunst in Osterreich, Vienna: melodies 15.18 and 16.59 from *Denkmäler der Tonkunst in Osterreich.*

Harvard University Press, Cambridge, MA: melody 13.84, reprinted by permission of the publishers from Willi Apel and Archibald T. Davison, *Historical Anthology of Music,* Vol. II, copyright 1946, 1949, 1950 by the President and Fellows of Harvard College.

H.W. Gray Co., New York, NY: melodies 3.47, 5.15, and 12.48 from *Folk Song Chanteys and Singing Games* by Charles Farnsworth and Cecil Sharp, reprinted by permission of Novello & Co., Ltd.

Louisiana State University Press, Baton Rouge: melody 6.11 from *Louisiana-French Folk Songs* by Irene Whitfield.

Mary O. Eddy, author of *Ballads and Songs from Ohio,* published by J.J. Augustin, Locust Valley, NY: melodies 3.40, 9.20 and 11.6.

Novello & Company, Ltd., London: melody 17.70 from *Caractacus* by Sir Edward Elgar, reproduced by permission.

University of Alabama Press: melodies 8.15 and 13.100 from *Folk Songs of Alabama* by Byron Arnold.

University of Utah Press, Salt Lake City: melody 14.54 from *Ballads and Songs from Utah* by Lester A. Hubbard, University of Utah Press, 1961.

Vermont Printing Company, Brattleboro: melody 17.57 from *Cancionero Español* by Maria Diez de Onate.

The illustrations on pages 2 and 299 were based on several online sources:

Gordon Lamb, "The Conducting Beat Patterns," Connexions, March 20, 2009, http://cnx.org/content/m20804/1.1/.

"What Do I See When I Look at the Conductor?," http://drribs.tripod.com.

"Conducting Course," The Church of Jesus Christ of Latter-Day Saints, 1992, http://www.lds.org/cm/ccourse/Lessons/ConductCourse33619000_06.pdf.

I would like to thank the following individuals for their suggestions as I prepared the manuscript for the ninth edition: Richard Hoffman (Belmont University), Keith Salley (Shenandoah University), Christine Linial (University of Texas at San Antonio), William Harbinson (Appalachian State University), James Hutchings (Carl Sandburg College), Danny Beard (University of Southern Mississippi), Jeffrey L. Gillespie (Butler University), and Jill T. Brasky (University of South Florida).

I remain grateful to Alan Theisen (Mars Hill College), who set all of the new melodies for this edition after doing a superb job of setting the entire eighth edition. William Wieland (Northern State University), who was a joy to work with, combined his expert musicianship and technological skills to design and implement the Rhythm Generator. I would also like to thank Roth Wilkofsky, Senior Publisher for Pearson Arts and Sciences, for his insightful advice and forward thinking. Joseph Scordato, Project Manager for Pearson Higher Education, oversaw the production of this book; he was unfailingly helpful when I had questions and worked diligently to solve problems before they arose. Last but by no means least, I am enormously indebted to my husband, Michael Buchler, for his constant personal and professional support.

Nancy Rogers

RHYTHM

Simple Meters;
The Beat and Its Division into Two Parts

The Rhythm Generator on MySearchLab
provides virtually unlimited rhythm-reading
exercises corresponding to this chapter.

An important attribute of the accomplished musician is the ability to "hear mentally"—that is, to know how a given piece of music sounds without recourse to an instrument. Sight singing, together with ear training and other studies in musicianship, helps develop that attribute. The goal of sight singing is the ability to sing *at first sight*, with correct rhythm and pitch, a piece of music previously unknown to the performer. Accomplishing that goal demonstrates that the music symbols on paper were comprehended mentally before being performed. In contrast, skill in reading music on an instrument often represents an ability to interpret music symbols as fingerings, with no way of demonstrating prior mental comprehension of the score.

To help you become proficient in sight singing, this text provides you with many carefully graded music examples. Beginning in this chapter, you will perform the simplest of exercises in reading rhythm, after which you will perform easy melodic lines that incorporate those same rhythmic patterns.

RHYTHMIC READING

In simple meters (also known as simple time), the beat is divisible into two equal parts; therefore, any note value so divisible can represent the beat. Most commonly used are the quarter note ($\decrescendo$ = $\decrescendo\decrescendo$), the eighth note ($\decrescendo$ = $\decrescendo\decrescendo$), and the half note ($\decrescendo$ = $\decrescendo$ $\decrescendo$), though other values (o, $\decrescendo$, $\decrescendo$) are sometimes seen. In this chapter, the note value representing the simple division of the beat (that is, half of the beat) will be the shortest note value used. In reading, follow these suggestions:

1. *Rhythmic syllables.* Accurate rhythmic reading is best accomplished through the use of spoken or sung rhythmic syllables. Any spoken method (even a neutral syllable) is preferable to clapping or tapping for a variety of reasons: dynamics and sustained notes are more easily performed vocally, faster tempos are possible, and vocalizing leaves the hands free for conducting. There are a variety of good rhythmic syllable systems in current use; several popular systems are illustrated in Appendix A.

2. *The conductor's beat.* The use of conductor's beats is highly recommended. Shown below are hand-movement patterns for two beats, three beats, and four beats per measure. Successive downbeats of each pattern coincide with successive bar lines. You should conduct with your right hand.

The Conductor's Beats: two beats, three beats, and four beats per measure

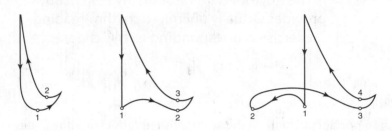

The *downbeat* (1) drops in a straight line and describes a small bounce at the instant the first beat occurs. The first downbeat is preceded by an *upbeat,* beginning at the point of the last beat of the pattern being used. Therefore, the last beat of each measure is the upbeat for the following measure.

Practice these three conductor's beats without reading or singing. Next, with the left hand, tap twice for each beat of the conductor's beat. These taps represent the normal simple division of the beat-note value. When you no longer have to concentrate on these hand movements, you are ready to begin rhythmic reading and sight singing.

3. *Striving for continuity.* It should be obvious that only the first performance of an exercise can be considered reading at first sight. (After that, you are practicing!) Therefore, on the first try, you should not stop to correct errors or to study what to do next. As you read an exercise, use the conductor's beat and tapping to keep going without pause until the very end. If you make a mistake, don't hesitate or stop; the next "1" (downbeat) will be the next bar line where you can pick up your reading and continue to the end. If you made errors or lost your place, you can review and practice in anticipation of doing better on the next exercise. Follow this procedure beginning with the very first exercises. Conducting and tapping easy exercises now is the best way to prepare yourself for the more difficult exercises to follow.

4. *Notation for rhythmic reading.* Exercises such as *a* on the following page are designed specifically for rhythmic reading and therefore use a simple one-line staff. However, reading rhythmic notation from a melodic line, as in example *b,* should begin as soon as possible. As seen in this pair of examples

(illustrated with one of many possible solmization systems), there is no difference in the resulting rhythmic performance.

The melodies of Chapters 2 and 3 include only the same type of rhythm patterns found in this chapter.

Section 1. The quarter note as the beat unit. Beat-note values and larger only: ♩ = 1 beat, ♪ = 2 beats, ♩. = 3 beats, ○ = 4 beats.

Not all exercises begin on the first beat of the measure. Determine the beat number of the first note before reading. If there is an anacrusis (i.e., a pick-up), silently count from the downbeat and enter on the appropriate beat.

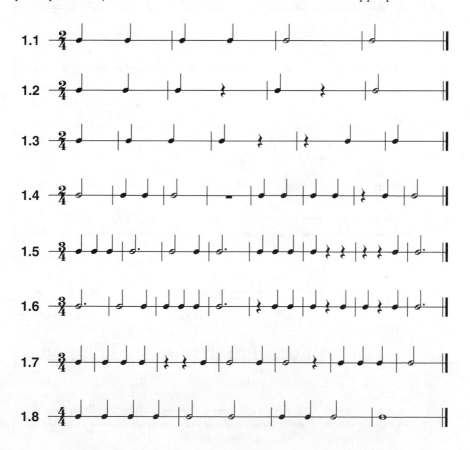

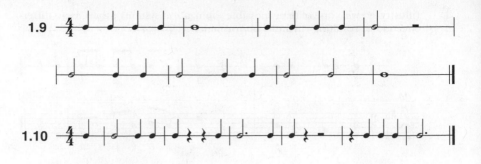

1.9

1.10

Section 2. The quarter note as the beat unit and its division ($\quad = \quad$).
Dotted notes and tied notes.

A tie connects two notes; simply continue the first note through the second without rearticulation ($\quad = \quad$). A dot extends the preceding note by half its value ($\quad = \quad$, $\quad = \quad$).

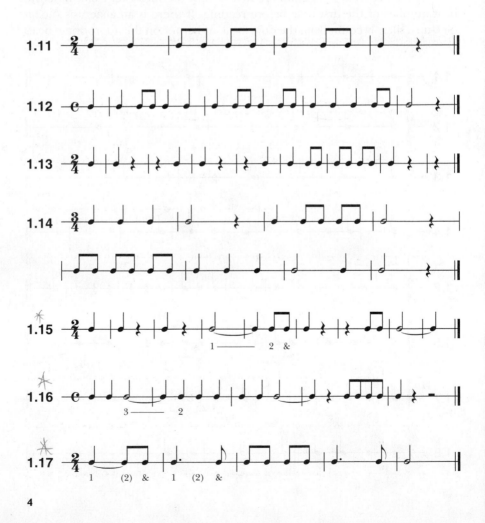

1.11

1.12

1.13

1.14

1.15

1 ——— 2 &

1.16

3 ——— 2

1.17

1 (2) & 1 (2) &

Section 3. Two-part drills.

Suggested methods of performance:

1. One person: Tap both lines, using both hands.
2. One person: Recite one line while tapping the other.
3. Two people: Each recite a line.

Only the meter signatures $\frac{2}{4}$, $\frac{3}{4}$, and $\frac{4}{4}$ will be found in melodies from Section 1 of Chapter 2. Sight-singing studies may begin there at this time.

Section 4. Note values other than the quarter note as beat values.

The half note, the eighth note, and the sixteenth note are also used to represent the beat. The signatures $\frac{2}{2}$ (¢), $\frac{3}{8}$, and $\frac{3}{8}$ are commonly used in written music. Others are occasionally seen. See Chapter 2, Section 3, for melodic examples of less common signatures.

In 1.30, examples *a, b, c,* and *d* all sound the same when the duration of each of their beat-note values ($\natural$, $\natural$, $\natural$, and $\natural$) is the same.

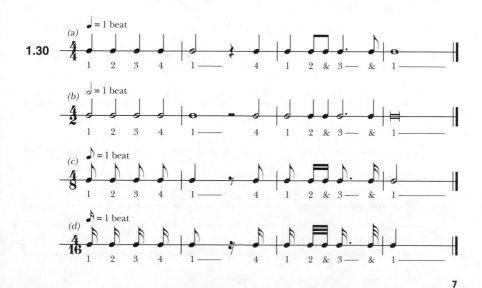

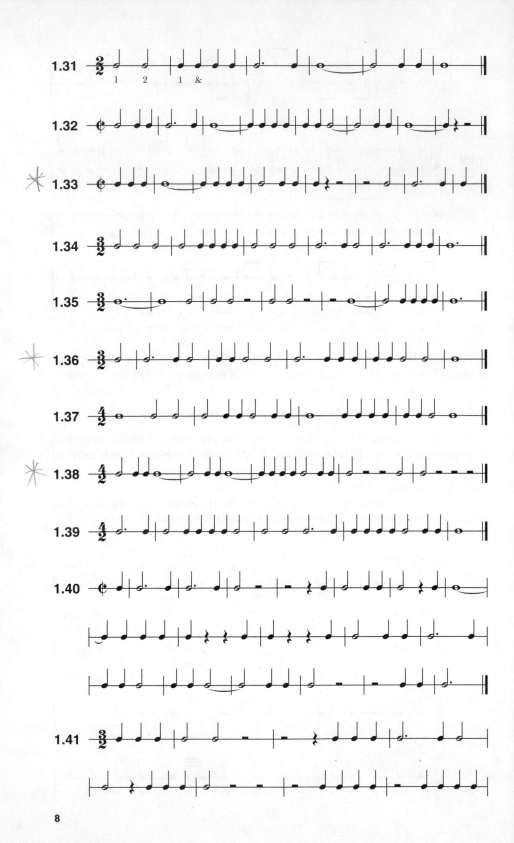

8

Section 5. Two-part drills.

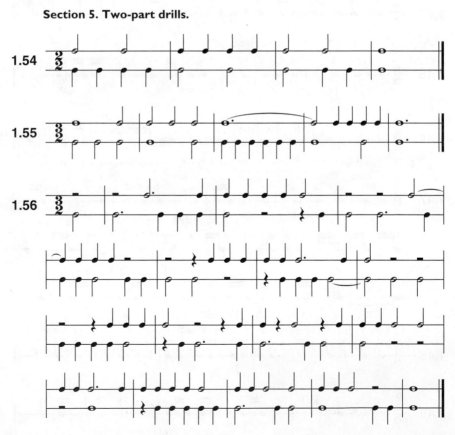

MELODY

Stepwise Melodies, Major Keys

RHYTHM

Simple Meters;
The Beat and Its Division into Two Parts

SIGHT SINGING

All melodies in Chapter 2 display stepwise movement and in a major key only; each interval is either a whole step (major second) or a half step (minor second).[1] If you can sing a major scale, these melodies should present very little difficulty.

Before reading a given melody, make these general preparations, all of which refer to later chapters in the text as well as to the melodies of this chapter.

1. Look at the key signature. What key does it indicate? On what line or space is the tonic? Does the melody begin on the tonic tone, or on some other pitch? (You may play the tonic note, but no other, immediately before singing.)

2. Scan the melody for passages in stepwise movement and then for larger intervals, particularly those presented in the chapter under study.

3. Observe the phrase marks. The end of a phrase mark usually indicates a cadence (that is, a temporary pause or a final stopping place), much the way commas and periods indicate pauses in language reading. Look ahead to the last note under each phrase mark so that you know where you are heading.

4. Firmly establish the key in your mind. Singing a scale is helpful, but many musicians prefer a more elaborate pattern such as the one below. (If the melody

---

[1] Most melodies in this chapter were written by Robert Ottman. The remainder of the text includes, for the most part, only folk music or music by recognized composers, but examples from these sources occur too infrequently for the purposes of Chapter 2.

goes significantly below the tonic, sing the lower note in measure 3; if it stays mostly above the tonic, sing the high note.)

5. Continue to use the conductor's beat, as described under "Rhythmic Reading" on page 2. Remember that "sight singing" refers only to the *first* time you sing the melody. Sing to the end of the example without stopping, no matter how many mistakes you make. Then go back, review the melody, practice the rough spots, and sing the entire melody again.

Pitch solmization for Western music has a venerable history, dating back approximately a thousand years to Guido d'Arezzo.[2] Its longevity is easily explained: with practice, most musicians find that solmization facilitates accurate sight singing. Several different systems are currently used:

1. Moveable-*do* solfège, where the tonic note is *do*
2. Scale-degree numbers, where the tonic note is $\hat{1}$
3. Letter names (already familiar to North American musicians)
4. Fixed-*do* solfège, where C is *do* even when C is not the tonic

A simple illustration is shown below; detailed information is provided in Appendix B.

Moveable-*do* solfège:	do	re	mi	fa	sol	la	ti	do
Scale-degree numbers:	$\hat{1}$	$\hat{2}$	$\hat{3}$	$\hat{4}$	$\hat{5}$	$\hat{6}$	$\hat{7}$	$\hat{1}$ (or $\hat{8}$)
Letter names:	G	A	B	C	D	E	Fis (F♯)	G
Fixed-*do* solfège:	sol	la	ti	do	re	mi	fa	sol

Section I. Major keys, treble clef, the quarter note as the beat unit. Key signatures with no more than three sharps or three flats.

Solfège:	do	re	mi	fa	sol		sol	fa mi fa	mi re	do
Scale degrees:	$\hat{1}$	$\hat{2}$	$\hat{3}$	$\hat{4}$	$\hat{5}$		$\hat{5}$	$\hat{4}$ $\hat{3}$ $\hat{4}$	$\hat{3}$ $\hat{2}$	$\hat{1}$
Letter names:	C	D	E	F	G		G	F E F	E D	C

⊗ indicates the location of the tonic note.

[2] Guido d'Arezzo was a Benedictine monk who lived from approximately 991 until some time after 1033 and wrote one of the most widely read music instruction books of the Middle Ages. The solmization system passed down from Guido is known today as solfége (or solfeggio).

14

2.9

mi
$\hat{3}$

2.10

2.11

2.12

2.13

mi fa so la so f so fa

2.14

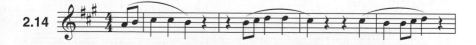

2.15

Melodies occasionally begin on pitches outside of the tonic triad, as in the next two examples. Be sure to identify the key first, then sing a scale from the tonic pitch up or down to the melody's first note. Alternatively, given that the first note necessarily falls within one scale step of $\hat{1}$, $\hat{3}$ or $\hat{5}$, it is also convenient to sing the nearest member of the tonic triad and then move stepwise to the first note of the melody. The latter strategy is depicted here.

2.16

Bb: (sol) la ti
       ($\hat{5}$) $\hat{6}$ $\hat{7}$

2.17

A: (mi) fa mi
      ($\hat{3}$) $\hat{4}$ $\hat{3}$

Section 2. Bass clef.

2.18

2.19

2.20

Do re mi re do ti la so   so la ti do re mi re   do

17

Section 3. Other meter signatures.

The meter signatures in melodies 2.32–2.40 are quite common. Review examples in Chapter 1, Section 4.

19

2.39

2.40

2.41

2.42

2.43

Section 4. Duets.

Suggested methods of performance:

1. Two people: Each sing a line.
2. One person: Sing one line while playing the other on the piano.

2.44

2.45

2.46

2.47

2.48

2.49

Section 5. Structured improvisation.

Structured improvisation exercises provide an opportunity to create your own melodies while practicing the skills addressed in each chapter. Sing the notes that are written, and complete the missing portions according to the guidelines provided (indicated by double arrowheads ➤➤ throughout the book). Notice that these exercises, unlike the more traditional rhythms and melodies in the earlier sections of this chapter, may be repeated multiple times because there are many different solutions.[3] (As an example, two distinct answers for exercise 2.50 are illustrated below; numerous other possibilities are left to your imagination.) It is highly recommended that you continue to use your preferred solmization system(s) while improvising.

➤➤ Using entirely stepwise motion, follow the suggested rhythm to fill in the missing notes.

2.50

Solution a:

Solution b:

➤➤ Using entirely stepwise motion and no rhythmic value shorter than an eighth note, complete the second phrase.

2.51

---

[3] You may even wish to repeat structured improvisation exercises after completing later chapters, in which case you will likely want to incorporate the new material you have learned. For instance, someone returning to the exercises in this chapter after finishing Chapter 3 might prefer to include some leaps from the tonic triad rather than using stepwise motion throughout.

➤➤ Choose a major key and a common simple meter. Using entirely step-wise motion and no rhythmic values shorter than the beat, improvise two four-measure phrases according to the following plan:

- Phrase #1 begins on $\hat{1}$, $\hat{3}$ or $\hat{5}$, and ends on the downbeat of measure 4 on $\hat{2}$.
- Phrase #2 ends on the downbeat of measure 8 on $\hat{1}$.

2.52

Begin on $\hat{1}$, $\hat{3}$, or $\hat{5}$ $\hat{2}$ $\hat{1}$
Any simple meter
Any key

Variation: work with a partner so that one person sings the first phrase and the other person sings the second phrase. Then try again with the roles reversed.

MELODY

Leaps within the Tonic Triad, Major Keys

RHYTHM

Simple Meters

The melodies of this chapter contain several intervals larger than the scale steps of Chapter 2. Singing these particular leaps will be relatively easy, since all are included in the tonic triad. If you can recognize and sing the three members of the tonic triad, you should have little or no problem when they occur in the melodies of this chapter.

In C major, the tonic triad is C E G; the possible intervals between any two of these pitches are as follows:

M = major, m = minor, P = perfect

The members of the C-major triad at *a* in the following exercise are arranged melodically at *b* and *c*. Sing these on scale-degree numbers or solfège syllables.[1]

[1] "R," "3," and "5" refer here to a triad's root, third, and fifth, respectively. In this chapter, these chord members coincide with $\hat{1}$, $\hat{3}$, and $\hat{5}$—that is, the first, third, and fifth scale degrees. See page 78 for an example of a nontonic triad.

Now add higher notes, lower notes, or both from the C-major triad and sing the new available intervals.

Here are successions of several leaps within the tonic triad, first in C major, then in several other keys. For each key, first sing $\hat{1}$-$\hat{3}$-$\hat{5}$-$\hat{3}$-$\hat{1}$, *do-mi-sol-mi-do,* or note names, carefully noting the location of each of these on the staff. You can see that if $\hat{1}$ (*do*) is on a line, $\hat{3}$ (*mi*) and $\hat{5}$ (*sol*) are on the next two lines above; or if $\hat{1}$ is on a space, $\hat{3}$ and $\hat{5}$ are on the two spaces above.

Pay particular attention to the unique sound of each of these members of the tonic triad. Memorize these sounds as soon as possible. Leaps among them are frequently used in other melodic or harmonic configurations.

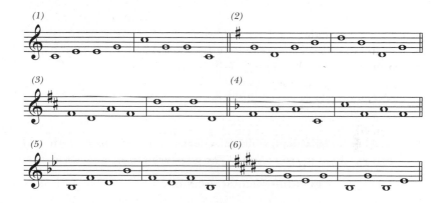

Now we are ready to sing melodies that include both stepwise motion and leaps within the tonic triad. Follow these steps in preparation for singing each melody:

1. Determine the key.
2. Spell the tonic triad.
3. Locate the tonic triad on the staff.
4. Scan the melody for examples of leaps within the tonic triad.
5. Sing the tonic triad.

Try this procedure on the following melody:

Note that:

1. The key is E♭ major.
2. The tonic triad is spelled E♭ G B♭.
3. The tonic triad is located on the first, second, and third lines. Also locate higher and lower tones of the triad on the staff.

4. Find leaps involving members of this triad.
5. Sing these intervals.

Section 1. Major keys, treble clef, leaps of a third, fourth, fifth, and octave within the tonic triad. The quarter note as the beat unit.

Key signatures in this chapter are limited to four sharps or flats until Section 6.

3.2 Moderato   Germany

3.3 Allegro   Bavaria

3.4 Moderato   Germany

3.5 Allegretto   Tennessee

3.6 Allegro   Poland

3.7 Allegro ... Spain
mf

3.8 Menuetto ... Haydn, String Quartet, Op. 3, No. 3

*♪ is a "grace note," to be sung as quickly as possible.

3.9 Allegretto ... Poland

3.10 Frisch ... Germany

Schubert, *German Dance*, D. 783, No. 7

3.11

3.12

Allegro   Germany

mf

f

3.13

Moderato   France

3.14

Allegretto   Germany

mp do re do so do re mi do mi fa so mi re do

so mi do mi do so mi do mi do mi fa mi re do

3.15

Vivo   Costa Rica

f

ff

[2] Review the text preceding melody number 2.16.

[3] This melody is from a collection in which Brahms set folk songs as vocal solos with piano accompaniment. Others will be found on later pages of this text.

Canon for 3 voices
P. Hayes (18th century)

3.22

Section 2. Bass clef.

3.23 Slowly France *p*

3.24 Allegro assai Mozart, Serenade, K. 237 *f*

3.25 Allegretto Germany *p* mi so la so fa mi re do ti la so *mf*
do
do ti la so fa mi so fa mi re do *p*

3.26 Allegro Germany *f* *mf* *f*

3.27 Allegro — Fr. Silcher (1842), *Alle Jahre wieder*

3.28 Allegretto — Spain

3.29 Allegro — Handel, *Judas Maccabaeus*

3.30 — Schubert, Waltz, D. 146, No. 8

3.31 Moderato — Spain

3.32 Lively · · · Spain

3.33 Allegro · · · France

Schubert, *Valse sentimental*

3.34

Section 3. Leaps of a sixth within the tonic triad.

3.35 Allegro · · · United States

3.36 Andante — Pomerania

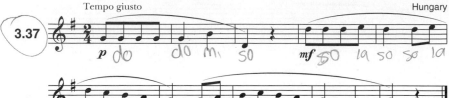

3.37 Tempo giusto — Hungary

3.38 Allegro — Mexico

3.39 Allegro moderato — Smetana, *The Bartered Bride*

3.40 Moderato — Ohio

Canon for 4 voices — Beethoven

3.41

Canon for 3 voices — England

3.42

Canon for 4 voices — P. Hayes

3.43

Section 4. The half note and the eighth note as beat units.

Andante — Slovakia

3.44

3.45 Adagio   Germany

3.46 Allegretto   Germany (Brahms)

3.47 Allegro   England

3.48 Stately   France

Section 5. Duets.

The asterisk (*) indicates the original folk song to which a second line has been added.

3.52 Germany

3.53 Andante con moto Germany

3.54 Allegro Germany

3.55

Largo non troppo

Germany

3.56

France

Section 6. Key signatures with five, six, and seven sharps or flats.

Although these key signatures occur less frequently, their use from the eighteenth century to the present is significant enough to warrant your attention. Bach used them in the two volumes of his *Well-Tempered Clavier* to demonstrate that any note of the chromatic scale could be used as a tonic. They were especially favored in the music of nineteenth-century Romantic composers such as Chopin, Brahms, Liszt, and Wagner.

If you find these key signatures alarming, consider that for the scale of every less familiar signature there is a more familiar scale occupying the identical lines and spaces of the staff. Shown here are the first five notes of the G♭-major scale (with six flats in the key signature) and the G-major scale (with one sharp in the key signature). Given that the two look alike on paper, obviously identifying 1̂, 3̂, and 5̂ is just as easy in G♭ major as it is in G major. Indeed, no key or clef is inherently more difficult to read than any other.

Make a conscientious effort to become familiar with different key signatures and clefs now so that you won't feel intimidated when they arise in later chapters, where the melodies will be more difficult.

3.59

Allegro   France

3.60

Allegro   Silesia

*(repeat **p**)*

3.61

Moderato   Silesia

rit.

3.62

Allegretto   Germany

41

3.63 Spain

Allegretto

pp do re mi mi so fa mi re

re mi re do ti la so do mi re do *pp*

3.64 England

Canon for 4 voices

1   2

3   4

3.65 Germany

Canon for 2 voices

1   2

3.66 Germany

Con spirito

*

3.67 Germany

Allegro
*

mf

mp < *mp* < *mf* >

Section 7. Structured improvisation.

➤➤ Complete the two phrases using only notes from the tonic triad. A suitable rhythm has been indicated.

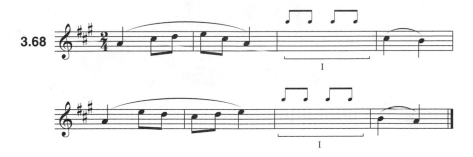

3.68

➤➤ Using only notes from the tonic triad, follow the suggested rhythm to complete the phrase.

3.69

➤➤ Following the given rhythm, use stepwise motion and leaps from the tonic triad (as indicated below each bracket) to complete the two phrases.

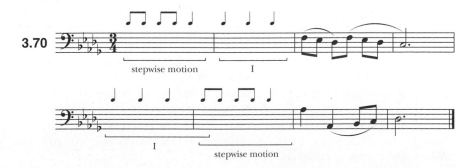

3.70

4

MELODY

Leaps within the Tonic Triad, Major Keys

RHYTHM

Compound Meters;
The Beat and Its Division into Three Parts

The Rhythm Generator on MySearchLab
provides virtually unlimited rhythm-reading
exercises corresponding to this chapter.

The melodies of this chapter include only those intervals already presented in Chapter 3. New to this chapter is the use of compound meter.

In compound meter, the beat divides into three parts and must therefore be represented by a dotted note. In $\frac{6}{8}$, for example, the dotted quarter note representing the beat is divisible into three eighth notes ($\downarrow. = \downarrow \downarrow \downarrow$). Dotted note values cannot be represented in traditional meter signatures, and so compound meter signatures must represent the beat indirectly by conveying the primary division of the beat. In $\frac{6}{8}$, there are six eighth notes per measure; three eighth notes together form one beat of a dotted quarter note, and a complete measure contains two beats (not six beats).

A meter signature with 6, 9, or 12 in its numerator is interpreted as representing a compound meter. It will ordinarily be conducted with two, three, or four beats per measure, respectively, and each beat will contain three rapid pulses (i.e., three divisions).

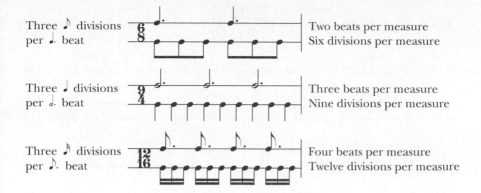

Three ♪ divisions per ♩. beat	Two beats per measure Six divisions per measure
Three ♩ divisions per ♩. beat	Three beats per measure Nine divisions per measure
Three ♪ divisions per ♪. beat	Four beats per measure Twelve divisions per measure

Some recent music conveys compound meter in a more straightforward manner. Instead of $\frac{6}{8}$, for example, the meter signature $\frac{2}{♩.}$ exactly describes the meter: two beats per measure with a dotted quarter note representing the beat. Similar, $\frac{3}{♩.}$ is equivalent to $\frac{9}{4}$, $\frac{4}{♩.}$ is equivalent to $\frac{12}{16}$, and so forth. Several good rhythmic solmization systems are in current use; please see Appendix A for descriptions and illustrations.

Melodies in compound meters are far less common than those in simple meters. Of the possible compound meter signatures, those with a numerator of 6 are the most frequently used. Sections 1 and 4, "Rhythmic Reading," in this chapter will include a variety of compound meter signatures. Compound triple and compound quadruple meters are rare in melodies at the level of this chapter. Melodies 4.51–4.54, written by Robert Ottman, use selected meter signatures to provide introductory practice.

Section 1. Rhythmic reading: The dotted quarter note as the beat unit. Single lines and two-part drills.

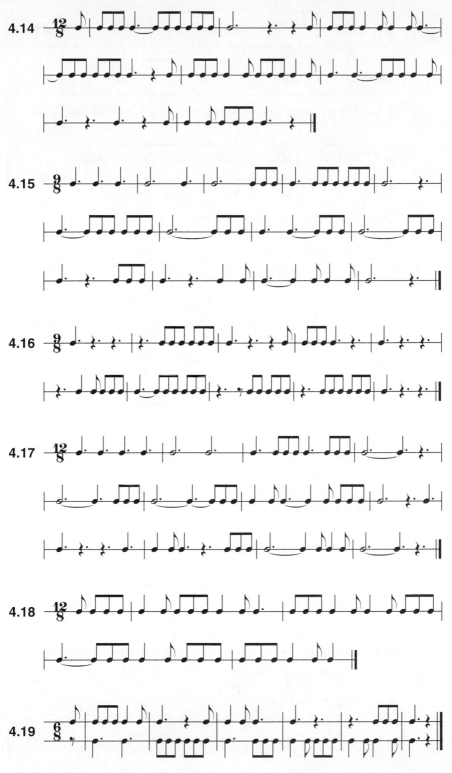

4.20

4.21

4.22

4.23

Section 2. Sight singing: Major keys, treble clef; the dotted quarter note as the beat unit.

49

4.29 Moderato   England

4.30 Allegro moderato   England

4.31 Lively   France

Canada

4.32

Fine

D.C. al Fine

4.33 Lightly England

4.34 Con moto England

Tchaikovsky, *The Queen of Spades*, Op. 68

4.35 Allegro vivo

4.36 Con spirito England

4.37 Con moto — United States

4.38 Rather slow — France

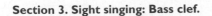

4.39 Allegretto — England

4.40 Vif — France

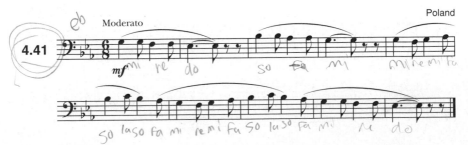

4.41 Moderato — Poland

4.42 Andantino — Missouri

4.43 Lively — Germany

4.44 Moderato — Missouri

4.45 Allegro — Germany

Handel, *L'Allegro*

4.46

France

4.47

France

4.48

55

4.54

Section 4. Rhythmic reading: The dotted half note and the dotted eighth note as beat units, including two-part drills.

In number 4.55, examples *a*, *b*, and *c* sound the same when the duration of their respective beat notes (♩., ♩., ♪) is the same.

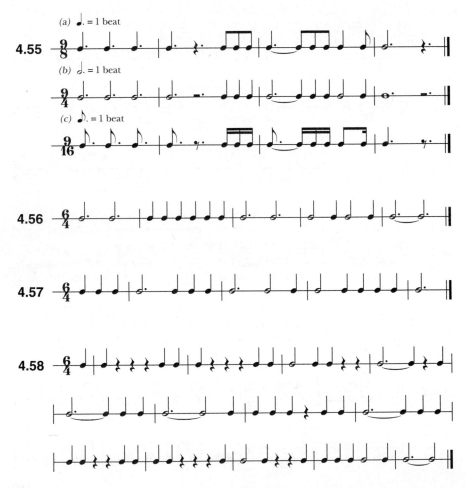

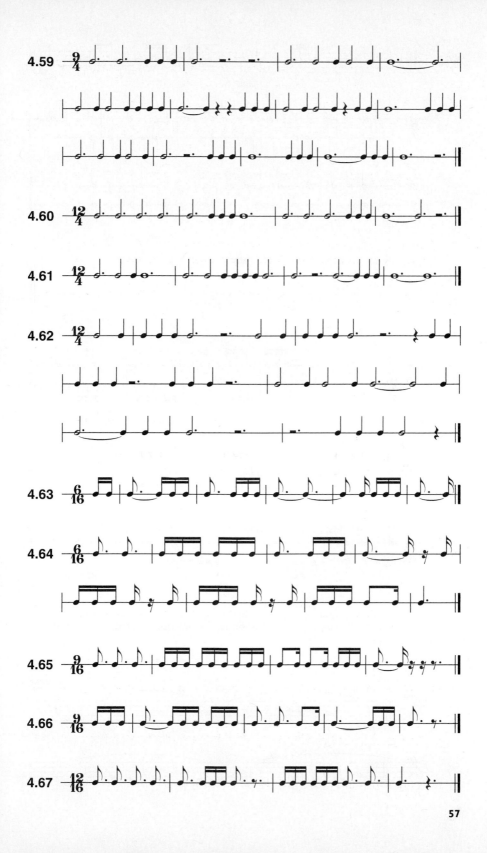

Section 5. Sight singing: The dotted half note and dotted eighth note as beat units.

Canon for 4 voices   W. Hayes (18th century)

4.75
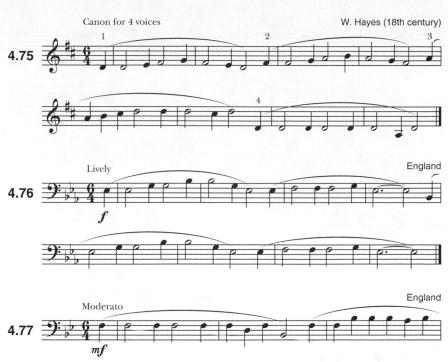

Lively   England

4.76

Moderato   England

4.77

Allegretto   France

4.78

Allegretto   Indiana

4.79

4.80

4.81

Section 6. Duets.

4.82

4.83

Andante

Spain

4.84

Con moto

Germany

4.85

Moderato comodo

England

Section 7. Structured improvisation.

➤➤ Use stepwise motion and leaps from the tonic triad (as shown below each bracket) to complete the phrase. A rhythm has been indicated for measure 2, but you should improvise your own rhythm for measure 4.

➤➤ In measure 1, notes have been provided, but you will need to improvise your own rhythm. Use any combination of ♪, ♩, and ♩. that fits the meter. In measure 3, use only notes from the tonic triad, improvising your own rhythm.

4.89

➤➤ Complete the melody with notes from the tonic triad, using any combination of ♪, ♩, and ♩. that fits the meter.

4.90

MELODY

Minor Keys; Leaps within the Tonic Triad

RHYTHM

Simple and Compound Meters

In minor keys, most melodic lines conform to the melodic form of the minor scale, using ↑$\hat{6}$ and ↑$\hat{7}$ (raised $\hat{6}$ and raised $\hat{7}$) when the line's continuation ascends and ↓$\hat{6}$ and ↓$\hat{7}$ (natural $\hat{6}$ and natural $\hat{7}$) when the line's continuation descends.[1] Most people who use moveable solfège consistently designate the tonic as *do* in both major and minor keys. However, others follow the earlier practice of designating the tonic as *la* in minor keys. People who sing using scale-degree numbers always identify the tonic as $\hat{1}$. For a more complete explanation of solmization in minor keys as well as a pronunciation guide, please consult Appendix B.

Follow these steps as preparation for sight singing in a minor key:

1. Be sure you can accurately sing the complete melodic minor scale in the key of the melody, both ascending and descending. Practice with letter names and with either numbers or syllables.
2. Look for examples of ↓$\hat{6}$ and ↓$\hat{7}$ and of ↑$\hat{6}$ and ↑$\hat{7}$. In general, ↓$\hat{6}$ and ↓$\hat{7}$ are likely to lead down to $\hat{5}$, while ↑$\hat{6}$ and ↑$\hat{7}$ are likely to lead up to $\hat{1}$.

G minor: ↑$\hat{7}$ ↑$\hat{6}$ ↓$\hat{6}$ ↑$\hat{6}$ ↑$\hat{7}$ ↑$\hat{7}$

[1] When a melodic line contains an ascending ↓$\hat{7}$, or ↑$\hat{6}$ without an accompanying ↑$\hat{7}$, that line is often based on one of the diatonic modes. See Chapter 20.

3. Note special uses of $\hat{6}$ and $\hat{7}$.

   a. In the succession $\hat{6}-\hat{7}-\hat{6}$, the direction of the last tone of this group determines which form of the scale is used for all three notes. See melody 5.3, measure 2. In the group B♭–C–B♭ ($\hat{6}-\hat{7}-\hat{6}$ in D minor) descends; therefore, all three notes are from the descending form of the scale.

   b. In the succession $\uparrow\hat{7}-\uparrow\hat{6}-\uparrow\hat{7}$, the direction of the last tone of this group determines that the ascending form of the scale is used for all three notes. See melody 5.3, measure 3. In the group C♯–B–C♯ ($\uparrow\hat{7}-\uparrow\hat{6}-\uparrow\hat{7}$ in D minor), the final C♯ ascends; therefore, all three notes are from the ascending form of the scale.

   c. The descending succession $\uparrow\hat{7}-\uparrow\hat{6}$ implies the use of dominant harmony at that point. In melody 5.9, the descending scale line A–G–F♯–E♮–D in G minor implies a V triad, A–F♯–D, with a passing tone between A and F♯ and between F♯ and A.

4. Recognize intervals. The same intervals used to construct a major triad are used to construct a minor triad. The perfect intervals (P4, P5, and P8) remain the same, but the major and minor intervals are reversed:

	Major Triad	*Minor Triad*
R up to 3	M3	m3
3 up to 5	m3	M3
3 up to R	m6	M6
5 up to 3	M6	m6
R up to 5	P5	P5
5 up to R	P4	P4

All intervals from the D-minor triad are here arranged melodically. Sing these on scale-degree numbers or solfège syllables.

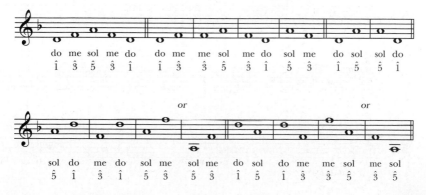

Here are successions of intervals from the tonic triad in various minor keys. Sing each group with numbers or with syllables.

Section 1. Simple meters.

5.1

$\hat{1}\hat{7}$ $\hat{1}\hat{7}\,\hat{1}\hat{6}$ $\hat{1}\hat{6}$ $\hat{1}\hat{6}\,\hat{1}\hat{7}$

do ti do re   do te le sol   fa sol le sol la ti do

5.2

a minor
do ti do te le so so la ti do re Me re do te le te so la ti do

5.3

d minor
do re me ti so le te le so fa so fa Me re do ti la ti do

$\hat{1}\hat{6}\,\hat{1}\hat{7}\,\hat{1}\hat{6}$ $\hat{1}\hat{7}\,\hat{1}\hat{6}\,\hat{1}\hat{7}$

5.4

g minor
so la ti do re me le do re me re me fa me re do ti do

5.5

c minor
do ti do te le so le so fa so le te le so

so le so la ti do ti do re Me re do

5.6

a minor
do re do ti do ti do te le so so la ti do re me re do ti do

66

5.12 Andante — Germany — *mp*

5.13 Canon for 4 voices — Haydn

5.14 Schubert, *Ecossaises*, D. 145, No. 1

5.15 Lent — France

5.16 Canon for 4 voices — England

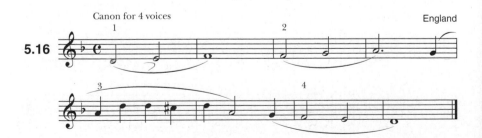

5.17

Adagio England

_mp_

_mf_

5.18

Slowly, with feeling Israel, _Midan Ad B'er Sheva_

so do re me fa so do me re do re me

do re me re me fa so do me re do ti do

5.19

Adagio Norway

_p_

_mp_ _pp_

5.20

Slowly Hebrew, _V'hi She'omdo_

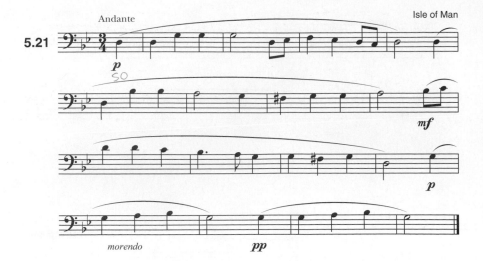

5.21 Andante — Isle of Man

5.22 Andante — Germany

5.23 Slow — Germany

5.24 Lento — Finland

5.25 Lentement   France

5.26 Lento   France

5.27 Lento   Wales

5.28
Gracefully and lively

Germany (Brahms)

5.29
Allegretto

Slovakia

5.30
Non troppo lento

Portugal

Section 2. Compound meters.

5.31
Andante

Basque

5.32
Vif

France

5.33 Andante   Wales

5.34 Allegretto   Wales

5.35 Joyeux   France

5.36 Allegro con grazia   England

5.37 Lento — France

5.38 Allegro — Italy

5.39 Larghetto — France

5.40 Allegro — England

5.41 Doloroso　　　　　　　　　　　　　　　　　　　　Germany

5.42 Adagio non troppo　　　　　　　　　　　　　　　　Germany

Section 3. Duets.

5.43 Joyeux　　　　　　　　　　　　　　　　　　　　France

5.44

Triste et lent

France

5.45

Adagio

France

5.46

Moderato

Slovakia

France

5.47

Tristement   France

5.48

Section 4. Structured improvisation.

▶▶ Complete this melody using stepwise motion and maintaining a constant eighth-note pattern until the last note. To help shape the melody, the first eighth note of every group (that is, the eighth note that falls on each beat) has been provided.

5.49

▶▶ Use stepwise motion and leaps from the tonic triad (as shown below each bracket) to complete the melody. A rhythm has been suggested.

5.50

▶▶ Improvise a second phrase using stepwise motion and leaps from the tonic triad. Restrict yourself to rhythmic values no shorter than an eighth note. As indicated, you should end with the tonic on the downbeat of measure 8.

5.51

6

MELODY

Leaps within the Dominant Triad (V);
Major and Minor Keys

RHYTHM

Simple and Compound Meters

Intervals from the dominant triad, very common in melodic writing, are the same as those from the tonic triad, but in a different context. In major keys, syllable names for members of the V triad are *sol–ti–re* (ascending), and the scale-degree numbers are $\hat{5}$–$\hat{7}$–$\hat{2}$, as at *a* and *b* below. Observe also that at *c*, its members can be identified as R–3–5 *of the triad.*

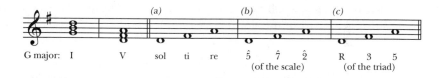

In minor keys, the dominant triad has the same sound as in major keys, since the leading tone is the *raised seventh* scale degree ($\uparrow\hat{7}$).

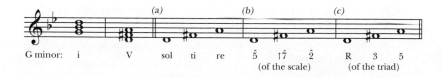

Observe these characteristics of the various possible intervals:

1. Leaps to the third of the triad (the *leading tone*) will soon become easy because, no matter how large the interval, the target note is always a half step below the tonic.

2. Leaps to the root of the triad are already somewhat familiar because this is $\hat{5}$ (the *dominant*) of the scale.

3. Leaps to the fifth of the triad will land a whole step above the tonic (*supertonic*).

Any leap within the dominant triad will be either to the dominant tone or to a scale step above or below the tonic tone, so remembering the sound of the tonic and dominant tones of the key (as learned in Chapters 3–5) is important.

Before singing, spell the tonic and dominant triads. Then scan the melody for leaps within the dominant triad. Example:

Observe that:

1. The key is G major. I = G B D.
2. The dominant (V) triad is D F♯ A.
3. At *a* (D down to A), the leap is to $\hat{2}$, the scale step above the tonic.
4. At *b*, the leaps outline the V triad.
5. At *c*, the interval, though large, is simply a leap to the leading tone, the scale step below the tonic.

Section 1. Leaps of a third within the V triad; major keys; simple meters.

6.1   Allegretto   Lithuania

p

mf (repeat *p*)

6.2   Moderato   Germany

p

mp

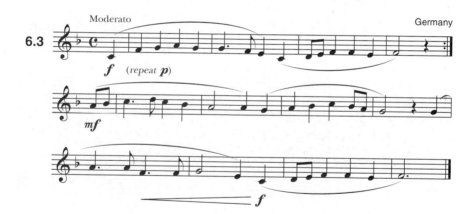

6.3   Moderato   Germany

f (repeat *p*)

mf

f

6.4   Andantino   Italy

f

1.   2.

81

Allegro   Germany (Brahms)

6.5

Moderato   England

6.6

Allegretto   France

6.7

Con spirito   England

6.8

Fine

D.C.

Canon for 4 voices   Germany

6.9

6.10 Lustily — Germany

f

6.11 Allegretto — Louisiana

mp

6.12 Moderato — Germany

mf

cresc.

f

Section 2. Leaps of a third within the V triad; minor keys; simple meters.

6.13 Allegro risoluto — Netherlands

f

6.14

6.15

6.16

6.17

Andante · Germany

6.18

Allegro assai · Mozart, *The Abduction from the Seraglio*, K. 384

6.19

Con moto · Netherlands

minor

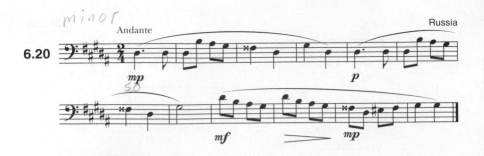

6.20 Andante — Russia

Section 3. Leaps of a fourth and fifth within the V triad; major and minor keys; simple meters.

6.21 Menuetto — Mozart, Symphony No. 15, K. 124

6.22 — Schubert, Minuet

6.23 Allegro spirito — France

6.24 Con moto — Germany

6.25

Andante — England

6.26

Allegro — Austria

6.27

Allegretto — Poland

6.28

Allegro — France

6.29

Slowly — Iceland

87

6.30   Canon for 2 voices   Germany

6.31   Canon for 2 voices   Wachsmann (1791–1853)

6.32   Canon for 3 voices   England

6.33   Ziemlich schnell   Schubert, *Erstarrung*, Op. 89, No. 4

6.34   Andante   Beranger, *Ce jour-là*

6.35

Ruhig · Germany

6.36

Lebhaft · Germany (Brahms)

minor

6.37

Moderato · Germany (Brahms)

6.38

Lento · Mexico

6.39 Andante — Germany

Section 4. Leaps of a sixth within the V triad; simple meters.

6.40 Allegretto — Dvořák, *Saint Ludmila*

6.41 Canon for 4 voices — Haydn

6.42 Andante — Russia

6.43 Andante — Germany

6.44 Moderato — Spiritual, United States

Section 5. Compound meters; various leaps within the V triad.

6.45 Allegro — France

6.46 Allegro — Germany

6.47 Quietly — Chile

6.52   Allegretto   Maine

6.53   Moderato   France

Section 6. Numerator of 3, compound meters.

Melodies with a numerator of 3 in the meter signature and with fast tempo indications are very often performed with a single beat per measure. The effect is that of compound meter, one beat per measure, as shown in the next four examples.

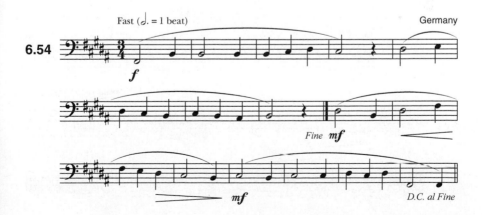

6.54   Fast (♩. = 1 beat)   Germany

Section 7. Duets.

6.60

Allegretto

Canada

6.61

Lentement

France

6.62 Allegro con brio — Netherlands

6.63 Allegretto — Sweden

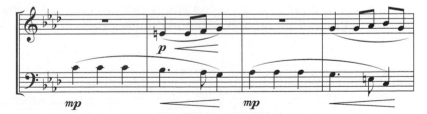

6.64 Andante — Netherlands

Section 8. Structured improvisation.

➤➤ Complete this melody using notes from the dominant triad. Suitable rhythms have been suggested in most places, but you will need to improvise your own rhythm in measure 7 (restrict yourself to rhythmic values no shorter than an eighth note).

6.65

➤➤ Complete this melody using notes from the tonic and dominant triads (as indicated below each bracket). A suitable rhythm has been suggested.

➤➤ Complete this melody using notes from the tonic and dominant triads (as indicated below each bracket). A suitable rhythm has been suggested.

THE C CLEFS

Alto and Tenor Clefs

The clef sign 𝄡, or less commonly 𝕂, indicates the location of *middle C* on the staff. When found on the third line of the staff, the C clef is known as the "alto clef," and when found on the fourth line, it is known as the "tenor clef."

alto clef   tenor clef

The alto clef is commonly used by the viola, the tenor clef by the cello, the trombone, and the bassoon, and each occasionally by other instruments. The ability to read music in these clefs is important, not only to the players of these instruments, but also to any musician studying orchestral scores such as those for symphonies, or chamber music scores such as those for string quartets. Vocal and instrumental music written before about 1700 freely uses these two C clefs, together with the soprano clef, the mezzo soprano clef, and the baritone clef (indicating F).

soprano clef   mezzo soprano clef   baritone clef

Section 1. The alto clef.

Before attempting to sight sing in any C clef, be sure to learn the names of the lines and spaces in that clef, just as you did when learning to read the treble and bass clefs. These are the names of the lines and spaces in the alto clef:

F   G   A   B   C   D   E   F   G   F   A   C   E   G   G   B   D   F

All of the melodies in this chapter use only those melodic and rhythmic materials already presented in previous chapters. To facilitate fluent clef reading, try singing melodies using the correct letter names. When singing in letter names, you may omit the words "sharp" and "flat" or use the modified German system explained in Appendix B to avoid changing the melody's rhythm. The melody *America* is written in alto and bass clef (melodies 7.1*a* and 7.1*b*); although the notation differs, the pitches are identical.

A♭ Major

7.9

Moderato — Germany
mf
so

Lively — Mexico

7.10
mp

f

D Major

Lively — Netherlands

7.11
f
so

1. 2.

Slowly — Hasidic, *My Candles*

7.12

E minor

7.13   Andantino   France
        mp
        50

        cresc.   *p*

7.14   Allegro   Germany
        f   *mp*

        mf   <

        <   *f*

7.15   Andante   Germany (Brahms)

        p.
        mi
        mf   *pp*   *p*

7.16   Vif   France
        f

        Allegro   Schubert, *Der Musensohn*, Op. 92, No. 1

7.17

        mf

7.18 Allegro — Italy

7.19 Allegretto — France

7.20 Moderato — Germany

Section 2. The tenor clef.

These are the names of the lines and spaces of the tenor clef:

D E F G A B C D E   D F A C E   E G B D

Also note that in the tenor clef, the first sharp of the key signature is on the second line, with the following sharps in the pattern fifth up and fourth down. This arrangement avoids the use of ledger lines.

After learning the names of the lines and spaces, sing with letter names the tune *America* as shown in melody 7.21. Its sound is identical to that of *America* in melodies 7.1*a* and 7.1*b*.

America

7.21

G G A F♯ G A B B C B A G A G F♯ G

Maestoso

Germany

7.22

f

D major

Allegretto

Germany

7.23

f

mp

rit.

7.29

Con moto

Germany

mf

dim.   *p*   *f*

7.30

Canon for 4 voices

Brahms

7.31

Andantino

Germany

7.32

Canon for 4 voices

Praetorius

England

7.33

E minor

Moderato   Purcell, *True English Men*

7.34

Section 3. Duets

Andante con moto   Germany

7.35

109

7.39

With vigor — England

Section 4. Additional practice in the C clefs.

Any melody in the treble or bass clef can be used for sight singing in either of the C clefs. We will again use *America* to demonstrate.

G   G   A   F♯   G A   B   B   C   B   A   G

1. Locate the line or the space of the tonic note. In *America* above, the tonic note is on the second line.

2. Ignore the given treble or bass clef, and imagine in its place an alto clef. With the alto clef, the second line is still tonic. Since the second line is A, the tonic is now A (or A♭). Add the appropriate key signature and sing the letter names in the key of A (A♭).

A   A   B   G♯   A B   C♯   C♯   D   C♯   B   A

3. In the tenor clef, the second line is F (or F#). Proceed as above. The key will be F (or F#). Sing the letter names in this key.

F   F   G   E   F G   A   A   Bb   A   G F

Section 5. Structured improvisation.

To increase your fluency reading alto and tenor clefs, try performing the exercises in this section using letter names.

▶▶ Complete this melody using notes from the tonic and dominant triads (as indicated below each bracket). You may wish to include passing tones and neighboring tones, but use rhythmic values no shorter than an eighth note.

7.40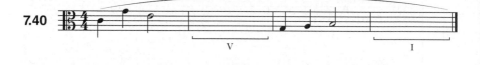

V   I

▶▶ Using mostly stepwise motion with occasional leaps from the tonic or dominant triad and no rhythmic value shorter than an eighth note, complete the second phrase.

7.41

▶▶ Using mostly eighth notes in stepwise motion with occasional leaps from the tonic or dominant triad, complete the second phrase. Try to create at least two good solutions, one in which the two phrases begins with the same notes and another in which the two phrases begins with different notes, or perhaps even a different contour. Repeat this exercise, but imagine that the alto clef has been replaced by a tenor clef (so that the first note is C rather than E).

7.42

MELODY

Further Use of Diatonic Leaps

RHYTHM

Simple and Compound Meters

Melodies from previous chapters have included the intervals most frequently used in melodic writing: major and minor seconds, major and minor thirds, major and minor sixths, the perfect fourth, and the perfect fifth. Intervals larger than the second were learned as used in tonic and dominant triads, contexts very frequently used and easy to read. This chapter presents the same intervals in different contexts.

For students correlating sight singing and harmonic studies, recognizing the particular use of an interval helps to achieve success in both areas. Here are new contexts you should be looking for.

1. Two successive leaps may outline a triad other than tonic or dominant. The subdominant and supertonic triads are those most frequently found in melodic form, as in melody 8.26 (IV triad) and melody 8.34 (ii triad). Look for the use of a different complete triad in melody 8.37.

2. Frequently you will encounter the easy third leap from $\hat{2}$ up to $\hat{4}$ or from $\hat{4}$ down to $\hat{2}$. Most often, this interval implies not the ii triad but the fifth and seventh of the V^7 chord, to be presented in Chapter 9. This interval is commonly found in melodies more difficult than those of the previous chapters.

3. A leap does not always imply a single harmony, even if the two tones are members of some triad. As an example, look at melody 8.33, which is notated below to reflect canonic performance. In the lowest voice, C up to F may look like the fifth up to the root of a V triad, or F down to B♭ may look like the fifth down to the root of a I triad. However, successive notes here are members of different triads. When taken out of context, the upper voice leaps from D to F and from B♭ to D may appear to constitute a tonic triad, but the second pair of notes is nonharmonic (appoggiaturas).

Before proceeding with this chapter, it will be very useful to learn to sing leaps from the ii and IV chords fluently. Leaps to $\hat{4}$ and $\hat{6}$ often require considerable practice, so don't become discouraged if you find them challenging initially. Several patterns providing these leaps within the context of a complete progression (tonic → pre-dominant → dominant → tonic) are provided below.

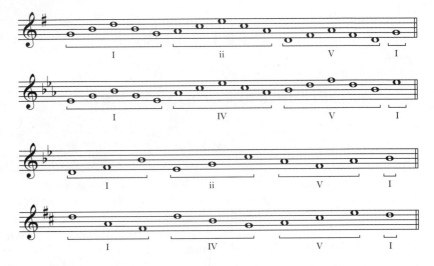

Suggestion: before singing, scan the melody to locate any less familiar leaps and concentrate on them specifically.

Section 1. Single-line melodies.

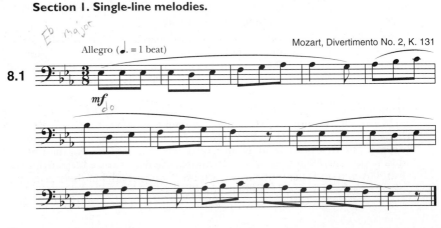

g# minor

8.2 Andante   Denmark

mf
50

rit.

8.3 Moderato   Yiddish, *Hammerl*

1.   2.

8.4 Canon for 3 voices   Haydn

1   2

3

8.5 Lento   France

mp   *Fine*

mf   *D.C.*

Ab major

8.12

Andante   Germany

mp

mi

8.13

Pas trop lent   France

pp

Db major

8.14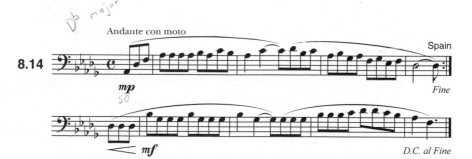

Andante con moto   Spain

mp

Fine

so

mf

D.C. al Fine

8.15

Allegretto   Alabama

f

8.20 Canon for 4 voices — Haydn

8.21 Allegro — England, *John the Miller*

When a melody seems to be woven from different strands in distinct registers (often described as a *compound melody* or *polyphonic melody*), it is usually best to focus on the continuity of the various strands rather than on the larger intervals that separate them. For instance, in melody 8.22 we may prefer to think of the F♯ in measure 2 as coming from the E in measure 1. Similarly, in melody 8.23 it is helpful to concentrate on the underlying stepwise descent C♯–B–A–G♯ in measures 3–4 and A–G♯–F♯–E in measures 7–8. Strategic use of close pitch connections beyond the note-to-note level will help you negotiate many otherwise difficult leaps successfully.

8.22 Allegro — Germany

8.23

Canon for 3 voices — Schubert

8.24

Allegro — Mozart, Symphony No. 10, K. 74

8.25

Allegro — Germany

8.26

Allegro — Pomerania

8.27

Con moto — Germany

8.28

Semplice — Finland

8.29

Con spirito — Germany

8.30

Langsam — Schubert, *Morgenlied*

8.31

Moderato — Schubert, *Der Entfernten*

8.32

Flowing

Yiddish, *In a Zumernakht*

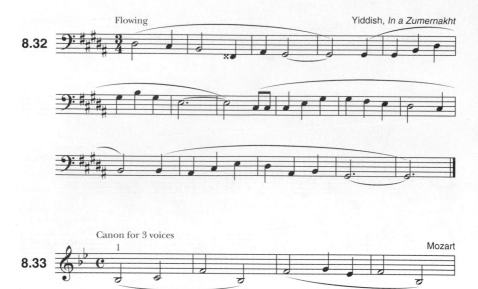

8.33

Canon for 3 voices

Mozart

8.34

Presto

Haydn, Symphony No. 100

p

8.35

Andante con molto di moto

Mendelssohn, *Das Schifflein*, Op. 99, No. 4

p

8.36 Moderato   *Germany*

p

8.37 Lento   Beethoven, String Quartet No. 16, Op. 135

p

8.38 Canon for 3 voices   *England*

8.39 Canon for 3 voices   *England*

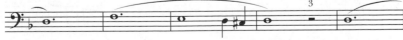

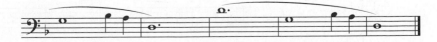

What triad is outlined by the first three notes of melody 8.43?

8.46

Allegretto — Argentina

8.47

Molto moderato — Spain

8.48

Allegretto — Poland

8.49

Allegretto — Yiddish, *Oifn Prijpetschik*

Section 2. Bass lines.

Some leaps tend to be associated with bass lines; they are particularly likely to occur before cadences. For instance, a leap from $\hat{1}$ to $\hat{4}$ (or $\hat{1}$–$\hat{6}$–$\hat{4}$) often leads to the cadential dominant, and successive leaps such as $\hat{1}$–$\hat{6}$–$\hat{2}$–$\hat{5}$–$\hat{1}$ or $\hat{1}$–$\hat{4}$–$\hat{2}$–$\hat{5}$–$\hat{1}$ are quite common. Mastering the characteristic patterns exemplified in excerpts 8.50–8.60 will help make other bass lines you encounter seem more familiar.

8.50 Bach, Chorale, *Jesu, der du meine Seele*

8.51 Allegretto — Haydn, Symphony No. 101

8.52 Andante, quasi Allegretto — Beethoven, Six Easy Variations, WoO 77

8.53 Andante — Schubert, Symphony No. 9

8.54 Bach, Chorale, *Ein Lämmlein geht*

8.55 Allegretto   Mozart, Piano Concerto No. 25, K. 503

8.56 Allegro e staccato   Handel, *Messiah*

Bach, Chorale, *Jesu meiner Seelen Wonne*

8.57

Bach, Chorale Prelude, *An Wasserflüssen Babylon*

8.58

8.59 Adagio   Corelli, Concerto Grosso No. 4

8.60 Allegro   Mozart, Piano Concerto No. 13, K. 415

Section 3. Duets.

8.61   Andante   Silesia

8.62   Adagio   England

8.63   Andantino   Latvia

Section 4. Structured improvisation.

Up until this point, you have been asked to outline specific triads simply by using their chord members exclusively (for instance, singing only $\hat{1}$, $\hat{3}$, and $\hat{5}$ for the tonic triad). However, it is possible—and, indeed, very typical—to convey a triad unambiguously even when notes outside the triad are also included. Stepwise motion between chord members is common, particularly when the chord members are emphasized through their metrical placement. As an illustration, three different elaborations of the tonic triad and one elaboration of the dominant triad are shown below.

As you will quickly realize, the number of distinct possibilities is virtually unlimited. The additional notes are frequently described as *passing* (if they connect two different chord members by step) or *neighboring* (if they connect two identical notes by step).

➤➤ Complete the next two melodies by singing elaborations of the triad indicated below each bracket. Suitable rhythms have been suggested.

➤➤ Create your own melody by improvising elaborations of the tonic, subdominant, and dominant triads (as indicated below each bracket). Use any combination of ♪, ♩ and ♩. that fits the meter, being sure to end with a suitably conclusive rhythm. (Helpful hint: before you begin, sing a simple arpeggiation of the underlying I–IV–V–I progression.)

8.69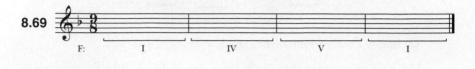

MELODY

Leaps within the Dominant Seventh Chord (V⁷); Other Diatonic Seventh Leaps

RHYTHM

Simple and Compound Meters

The dominant seventh chord is a four-note chord: the dominant triad plus an additional minor seventh above its root. Of all the possible intervals from this chord, these have not previously been presented:

Root up to seventh or seventh down to root = minor seventh (m7)

Third up to seventh or seventh down to third = diminished fifth (d5), or tritone[1]

Seventh up to third or third down to seventh = augmented fourth (A4), or tritone

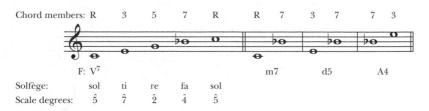

Chord members:	R	3	5	7	R		R	7	3	7	7	3

F: V⁷   m7   d5   A4

Solfège:		sol	ti	re	fa	sol
Scale degrees:		$\hat{5}$	$\hat{7}$	$\hat{2}$	$\hat{4}$	$\hat{5}$

Actively imagining the sound of the V⁷ chord will make these dissonant leaps much easier to sing.

---

[1] The term *tritone* refers to an interval composed of three whole steps—technically an A4. Because the d5 is enharmonic with the A4, it is also frequently described as a tritone.

133

Section 1. The complete dominant seventh chord.

In this section, successive chord tones outline a complete four-note V^7 chord or the near-complete V^7 chord (chord members R–5–7 or reverse), all utilizing only the intervals of the major third, the minor third, and the perfect fifth.

Section 2. The leap of a minor seventh within the V⁷ chord.

Before singing, plan the best way to negotiate each seventh leap. Will you imagine leaping an octave and then moving by step? Might you think back to a previous note in the same register? Are you leaping to a note that you can reliably find, regardless of context?

Fine **f**

D.C.

9.12 Andante — Germany

p   **mp**

p   **pp**

9.13 ♩. = One beat — Mexico

f

< ff

f

mf

9.14 Canon for 4 voices — England

1   2

3   4

9.15 Canon for 3 voices — Germany

9.16 Allegro — Germany

9.17 Haydn, Divertimento

Fine

D.C.

9.18 Allegro — France

Fine

D.C.

Canon for 4 voices — Mozart

Section 3. The leap of a tritone within the V⁷ chord.

Many of the leaps in melody 9.22 will be much easier if you think about the compound melodic implications (see page 119).

9.26 Moderato ma con moto — Poland

9.27 Allegro — Mexico

9.28 Nicht schnell — Schumann, *Blondels Lied*, Op. 53, No. 1

9.29

Mutig

Germany

9.30

Allegro ma non troppo

Germany

9.31

Allegretto e marcato

Germany

Section 4. Other diatonic seventh leaps.

How might we most easily find the F in measure 2?

9.34

Allegro

Haydn, Piano Sonata in E♭ Major (1780)

9.35

Canon for 3 voices

Purcell

9.36

Adagio

Rachmaninoff, Symphony No. 2

9.37

Lightly

England

Allegro

9.38

Section 5. Structured improvisation.

▶▶ Complete this melody using notes from the tonic triad and dominant seventh chord (as indicated below each bracket). Restrict yourself to rhythmic values no shorter than an eighth note.

9.39

▶▶ Complete this melody using elaborations of the tonic triad and dominant seventh chord (as indicated below each bracket). Use any combination of ♪, ♩, and ♩. that fits the meter.

9.40

▶▶ Complete this melody as indicated below each bracket. Include at least one leap of a minor seventh (between $\hat{5}$ and $\hat{4}$ either ascending or descending) both in measure 2 and in measure 5. Restrict yourself to rhythmic values no shorter than an eighth note and no longer than a half note.

9.41

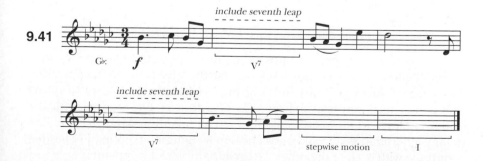

145

RHYTHM

The Subdivision of the Beat:
The Simple Beat into Four Parts,
The Compound Beat into Six Parts

The Rhythm Generator on MySearchLab
provides virtually unlimited rhythm-reading
exercises corresponding to this chapter.

RHYTHMIC READING, SIMPLE METERS

In simple meters, the beat may be subdivided into four parts. Three illustrations appear below.

$$\frac{2}{4} \ \ \quad = \quad \qquad \qquad \frac{2}{2} \ \ \quad = \quad \qquad \qquad \frac{3}{8} \ \ \quad = \quad$$

There are a variety of good rhythmic syllable systems that reflect the subdivided beat. Several popular systems are presented in Appendix A; you may wish to use another approach.

Section I. Preliminary exercises, simple meters.

Following are three groups of patterns, one each for the subdivisions of the ♩, ♩, and ♪ notes. Select first the group under the heading "♩ = 1 beat." Read each line in the group, repeating without interrupting the tempo until you have mastered it. Continue in like manner with the following line. When you have completed all the lines, skip from one line to any other line, as directed or as chosen, without interrupting the tempo. Continue with each of the other two groups in this same manner.

The patterns shown are those most commonly used. The rhythmic figures ♪♩. and ♪♪♩ (and comparable figures for other beat values) will be presented in Chapter 13, "Syncopation."

Section 2. Rhythmic reading exercises in simple meters.

148

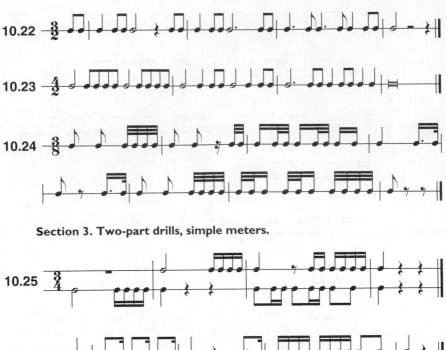

Section 3. Two-part drills, simple meters.

RHYTHMIC READING, COMPOUND METERS

In compound meters, the beat may be subdivided into six parts. Three illustrations appear below.

Again, there are a variety of good rhythmic syllable systems that reflect the subdivided beat. Several popular systems are presented in Appendix A; you may wish to use another approach.

Section 4. Preliminary exercises, compound meters.

Follow directions for similar exercises in simple meters, page 146. The patterns in subdivision shown are the most common of those possible. Notice that beaming styles may vary.

= 1 beat
(beat) 1.
(division) 2.
(subdivision) 3.
4.
5.
6.
7.
8.
9.
10.
11.

= 1 beat
1.
2.
3.
4.
5.
6.
7.
8.
9.
10.
11.

= 1 beat
1.
2.
3.
4.
5.
6.
7.
8.
9.
10.
11.

Section 5. Rhythmic reading exercises in compound meters.

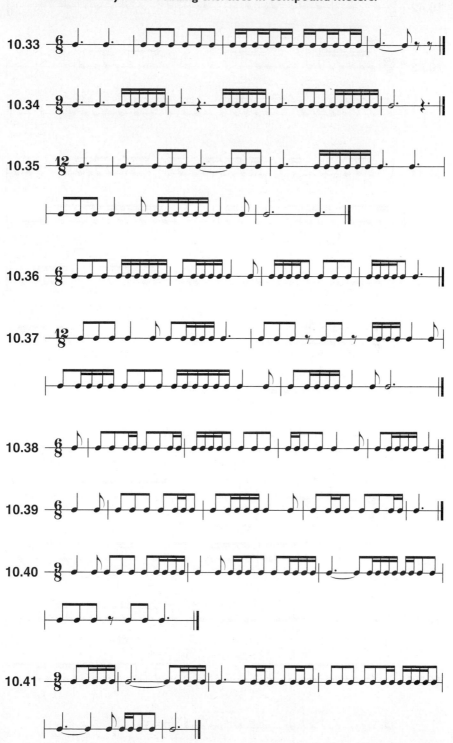

10.60

10.61

10.62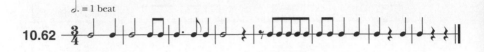

10.63

10.64

Section 6. Two-part drills, compound meters.

10.65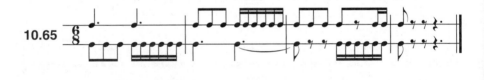

10.66

10.67

10.75

10.76 ♩. = 1 beat

10.77 ♩. = 1 beat

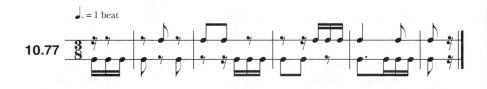

10.78 ♩. = 1 beat

10.79

MELODY

Leaps within the Tonic and Dominant Triads

RHYTHM

Subdivision in Simple and Compound Meters

Section 1. Single-line melodies and duets.

Reichart, *Wär ich ein wilder Falte*

11.1 Moderato

Brisk — Spain

11.2

11.3

Moderately   Yiddish, *Bulbe*

11.4

Allegretto   Yiddish, *Jome*

11.5

Con moto   England

11.6

Andante   Ohio

11.7

Andante con moto — Ukraine

11.8

Vif et gai — France

11.9

Allegretto — France

Fine

f (repeat *p*)

D.C. al Fine

Hasidic, *Shiru Ladonoi*

11.10

11.11

Tres vif

France

11.12

Canon for 3 voices

Beethoven

11.13

Allegro non troppo

Italy

11.14

Canon for 3 voices

Hebrew, *Hashivenu*

11.15

Langsam

Schubert, *Wiegenlied*, D. 498

pp

11.16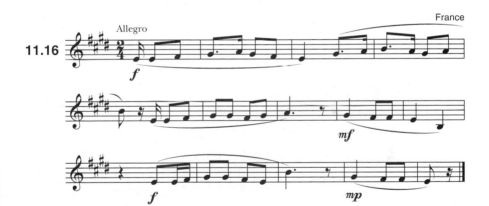

Allegro

France

f

mf

f

mp

11.17

Allegro

Spain

f

11.18
Lent   France

11.19
Allegro   Russia

11.20
Dolendo   Nicaragua

11.21
Canon for 3 voices   England

11.22
Con moto   Texas

11.23
Andante moderato   Germany

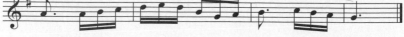

11.24 Allegro — England

Canon for 4 voices — Germany

11.25

Andante — Scotland

11.26

11.27 Canon for 4 voices   1   2   3   4   England

11.28 Andante   England

mp

mf

11.29 (Stately)   Handel, *Teseo*

mf *cresc.*   *f*

11.30 Mesto   Ukraine

11.31 Andantino   Italy

mf

cresc.

11.32 Moderato *Russia*

Section 2. Structured Improvisation.

➤➤ As indicated below each bracket, fill in the missing beats with an out-line of the tonic triad, an outline of the dominant triad, or stepwise motion. A rhythm has been suggested in most places, but you will need to improvise your own rhythm in measure 7.

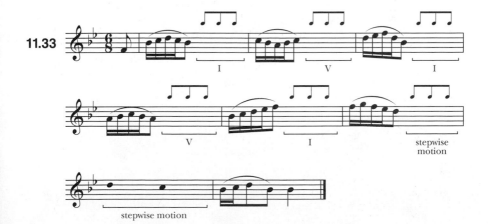

11.33

➤➤ A melodic outline for two phrases is provided below; notice that the two cadential measures have been completed. Using entirely stepwise motion and any combination of ♪ and ♩ that fits the meter, connect these notes (all of which fall on the beat) so that they form a complete melody. Look over the entire exercise and think about the key before you begin.

11.34

➤➤ Improvise a second phrase that "answers" the first (in other words, improvise a consequent phrase to the given antecedent phrase). It is appropriate for the second phrase to sound similar to the first phrase, perhaps even using an identical beginning. However, the final cadence must sound more conclusive.

11.35

MELODY

Further Use of Diatonic Leaps

RHYTHM

Subdivision in Simple and Compound Meters

Section 1. Diatonic leaps except the seventh and tritone.

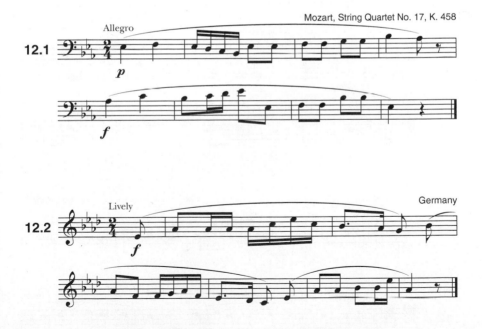

12.3 Lively — Yiddish, *Az der Rebbe Est*

12.4 Allegro molto — Cimarosa, *Il matrimonio segreto*

12.5 Poco allegretto — Lithuania

12.6 March merrily — Yiddish, *Khabad*

12.7 Allegro — France

Fine

D.C. al Fine

Allegro (♩. = 1 beat)   Stamitz, Concerto for Cello

12.8

Canon for 3 voices   J. Hilton (17th century)

12.9

Alla marcia   Germany

12.10

f *marcato*

12.11 Allegro — Mozart, *The Magic Flute*, K. 620

12.12 Gaiment et coulé — Couperin, *Les Dars-homocides*

12.13 England

12.14

Andante

Germany (Brahms)

p

12.15

Con moto

Gounod, *Dites, la jeune belle*

p

12.16

Andantino

Mozart, Divertimento No. 14, K. 270

p

12.17

Canon for 3 voices

Wm. Lawes

1

2

3

12.18

Giojoso

Serbia

f

12.19 Canon for 2 voices

Germany

12.20 Moderato

Haydn, Symphony No. 100

12.21 Con moto

Germany (Brahms)

12.22 Con dolore

Scotland

12.23 Bach, *Brandenburg Concerto No. 2*

12.24 Moderato — Argentina

12.25 Teneramente — Stephen Foster, *The Village Maiden*

Grieg, *Holberg Suite*, Op. 40

12.26 Allegretto

12.27 Allegretto Alabama

12.28 Adagio Rimsky-Korsakov, *The Snow Maiden*

12.29 Andante Mozart, *Cosi fan tutte*, K. 588

12.30 Couperin, *Soeur Monique*

Tendrement sans lenteur

12.31 Germany

Andante

Bach, Motet, *Jesu, meine Freude*

Section 2. Leaps of a seventh or tritone within the V⁷ chord.

12.42   ♩. = 1 beat   Swabia

Fine **mf**

D.C. al Fine

12.43   Andante   Jackson, *When a Woman*

12.44   Energico   Poland

12.45   Allegretto   Ukraine

12.46 Lively — France — *Fine* — *D.C. al Fine*

12.47 Andante con moto — Mendelssohn, *Songs Without Words*, Op. 53

12.48 Con moto — England

12.49 Andante — Arlberg (1830–1896), *Svärmeri*

12.50 Allegro — Martinique

12.51 Moderato, con brio — Purcell, *O How Happy's He*

12.52 Allegro — Handel, *Judas Maccabaeus*

12.53 — Ballade — Yiddish, *Proletarke, Schvester Mayne*

12.54 — Largo — Poland

Section 3. Other melodic dissonances.

12.55 — Mässig — Schubert, *Erntelied*

12.56 — Schnell — Germany

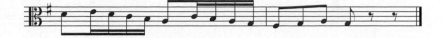

The melodic augmented second is unusual in common-practice music; in measure 3 of melody 12.60, it arises as an embellishing tone to the overall V^7 harmony. However, augmented seconds are quite common in some musical traditions. Melodies 12.61 and 12.62 are properly understood as ending on $\hat{1}$ (they employ an Ashkenazic mode that has a half step between $\hat{1}$ and $\hat{2}$), but thinking of the final note as $\hat{5}$ in a harmonic minor scale will enable you to find the right intervals.

12.60 Con tristezza   Russia

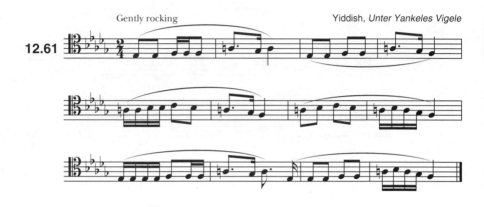

12.61 Gently rocking   Yiddish, *Unter Yankeles Vigele*

12.62 Vivace   Yiddish, *Maydelekh un Vaybelekh*

Section 4. Structured improvisation.

➤➤ A melodic outline is provided below. Using entirely stepwise motion and any combination of ♪ and ♩ that fits the meter, connect these notes (all of which fall on the beat) so that they form a complete melody.

➤➤ Complete this melody, incorporating the opening neighbor-note motive as often as possible. Try to sustain a rhythm of steady sixteenth notes until the very end (where it is appropriate to use a longer note that falls on a beat).

➤➤ Complete this melody, frequently including the opening motive (both the rhythm and the use of passing tones). Create an effective half cadence at the end of the first four-measure phrase and an authentic cadence at the end of the second four-measure phrase.

RHYTHM AND MELODY

Syncopation

The Rhythm Generator on MySearchLab
provides virtually unlimited rhythm-reading
exercises corresponding to this chapter.

Syncopation occurs when the normal metrical pattern of accentuation is deliberately contradicted. Syncopation can be created by

  1. Accenting a weak beat or a weak part of a beat:

  2. Tying a weak beat into the next strong beat:[1]

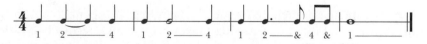

  3. Tying the weak division of a beat into the next beat:

[1]Some passages seemingly in syncopation may be subject to a different interpretation. For example, the pattern ♩ ♪♪♪♪|♩♪♪♪♪| is often performed as ♩ ♩ ♩♩|♩ ♩ ♩♩|, a device known as *hemiola*. See Chapter 17, page 305.

RHYTHMIC READING

Section 1. Syncopation in simple meters at the beat or beat division level.

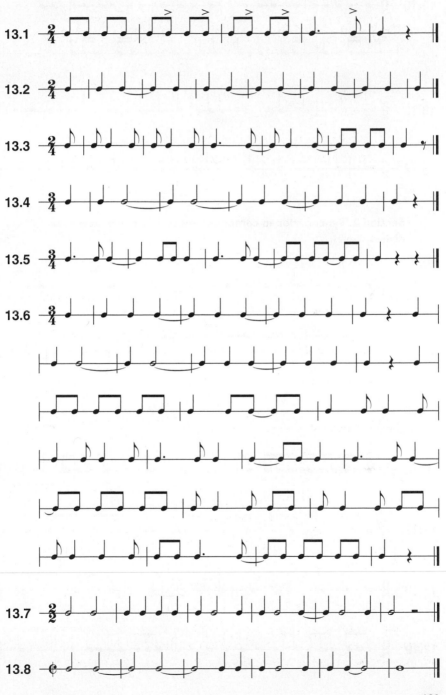

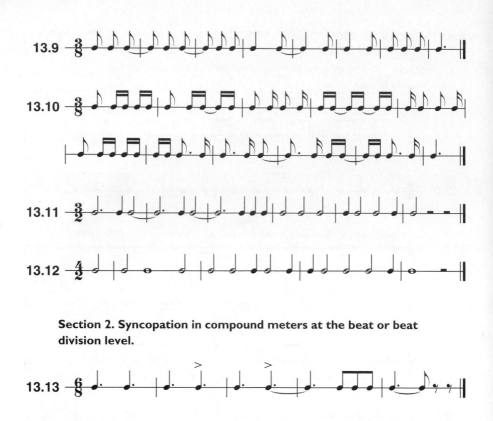

Section 2. Syncopation in compound meters at the beat or beat division level.

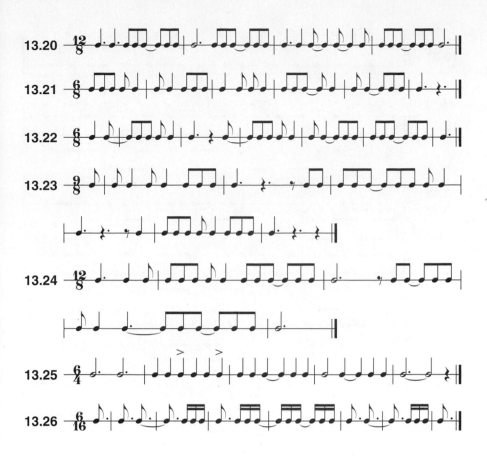

Section 3. Two-part drills.

13.31

13.32

13.33

13.34

13.35

13.36

13.37

13.38

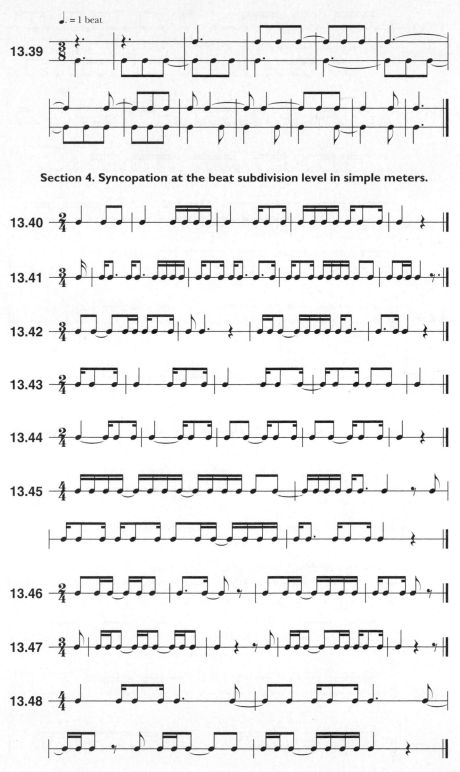

Section 4. Syncopation at the beat subdivision level in simple meters.

Section 5. Syncopation at the beat subdivision level in compound meters.

Section 6. Two-part drills.

SIGHT SINGING

Section 7. Syncopation in simple meters at the beat or beat division level.

13.71

Yiddish, *Wie asoj kenn ijch lustig sain?*

13.72

Allegro   Czechoslovakia

13.73

Allegretto   Schubert, Waltz, D. 145, No. 1

13.74

Tempo di menuetto   Mozart, Sonata No. 4 for Violin and Piano, K. 304

13.75   Moderato   Haydn, *Theresienmesse*

13.76   With spirit   Hebrew, *Hevenu Shalom Aleichem*

13.77   Andante   Spiritual, United States

13.78   Allegro   Piccini, *Allesandro nelle Indie*

13.79   Allegretto   Dominican Republic

13.80   With spirit   Hebrew, *Shuru Habitu*

13.81   Allegro assai   Haydn, Divertimento

13.82   Andante   Spiritual, United States

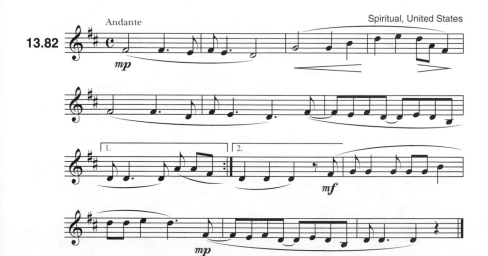

13.83 Allegro ♩. = 36 — Beethoven, String Quartet Op. 18, No. 6

13.84 Allegro — Muffat (1690–1770), Suite for Harpsichord

13.85 Poco allegretto — Romania

13.86 Allegro moderato — Mozart, Symphony No. 14, K. 114

13.87 Canon for 3 voices — Caldara

13.88 Haydn, Symphony in F# Minor (1772)

Adagio

13.89 Vivaldi, Concerto in C Minor for Two Violins

Allegro

13.90 Dowland, *Woeful Heart*

Slowly

Vivaldi, Concerto in G Minor for Two Violins

13.91

Section 8. Syncopation in compound meters at the beat or beat division level.

In the rhythmic figure ♪♩, the strong beat (first note) is usually accented, as in melody 13.92, measure 1 (similar to ♫., the so-called *Scotch snap* in simple meters). If the second note of the figure is to be accented, it is marked with a sign such as > or *sf*, as in melody 13.94.

Moderato   England

13.92

mf

Flebile   Mexico

13.93

13.94

$\downarrow. = 88$

Beethoven, String Quartet, Op. 18, No. 6

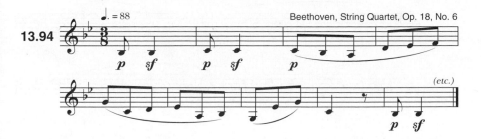

p *sf* *p* *sf* *p*

(etc.)

p *sf*

13.95

Vivo

Venezuela

f

p

f

f

13.96

Lilting

Hebrew, *Lo Vayom V'lo Valaila*

1.   2.

13.97

Assai agitato $\downarrow. = 126$

Schumann, String Quartet, Op. 41, No. 3

p

Section 9. Syncopation at the beat subdivision level in simple and compound meters.

13.102 Moderato

Florida

13.103 Allegro

Texas

13.104 Allegro

South Carolina

13.105 Giocoso

Haiti

Fine

D.C.

13.106

Moderato

(♩ ♫ ♫ ♫)

Cuba

13.107

Allegro

Spiritual, United States

13.108

Andante

Ireland

13.109

Moderately fast

Spiritual, United States

13.110 Andante grazioso   Scotland

13.111 Con moto   Trinidad

Fine *f*   *D.C.*

13.112

Lively

Cuba

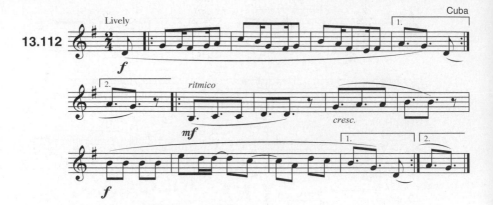

13.113

Allegro non troppo

Puerto Rico

13.114

Allegro

Spiritual, United States

13.115

Allegretto

West Indies Calypso

mf

f

mf

mp

Section 10. Duets.

13.116

Allegretto

Bohemia

mf

f

Fine

D.C. al Fine

13.117

Con spirito

Jamaica

13.118

Allegro

Haydn, String Quartet, Op. 20, No. 6

sempre sotto voce

Section 11. Structured improvisation.

➤➤ Maintaining the syncopated rhythm established in the opening measures, complete this melody by outlining the chords indicated below the brackets.

➤➤ Complete the melody below using syncopated rhythms like the one provided in measure 1. You may simply outline the triads indicated, or you may elaborate them with passing and neighboring tones.

➤➤ Improvise a consequent phrase that "answers" the given antecedent phrase. It is appropriate for the second phrase to sound similar to the first phrase, perhaps even using an identical beginning. However, the final cadence must sound more conclusive.

RHYTHM AND MELODY

Triplet Division of Undotted Note Values; Duplet Division of Dotted Note Values

The Rhythm Generator on MySearchLab provides virtually unlimited rhythm-reading exercises corresponding to this chapter.

A triplet division of an undotted note value is indicated by three notes with a "3" added. The division of three uses the same note value as that for the usual division into two parts (for example, ♩ = ♫ = ♫♫).

Triplet Division

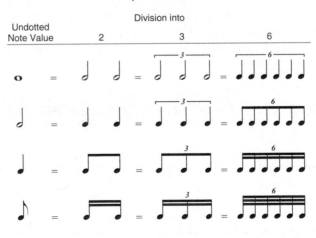

The duplet division of a dotted note can be indicated in three ways:

1. Most commonly, two notes with a "2," using the same note value as the division of three (♩. = ♫♫ = ♫).

2. Less commonly, two notes with a "2," using the same note value as the one being divided ($\downarrow$ = $\overset{2}{\downarrow\downarrow}$). See melody 14.63, shown as $\overset{4}{\downarrow\downarrow\downarrow\downarrow}$ (= $\overset{2}{\downarrow\downarrow}\overset{2}{\downarrow\downarrow}$).

3. Found mostly in twentieth-century music, two dotted notes of the next smaller value ($\downarrow$. = $\downarrow$. $\downarrow$. and $\downarrow$. = $\downarrow$. $\downarrow$.). An example of $\downarrow$. = $\downarrow$. $\downarrow$. can be seen in melody 21.61, among others, in Chapter 21.

Duplet Division

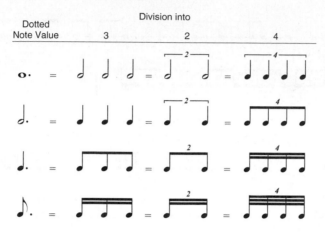

Division into

Dotted Note Value   3   2   4

RHYTHMIC READING

Section 1. Triplet division of undotted note values.

In example 14.1, *a* and *b* sound identical when performed at the same tempo. The triplet in simple meter could be said to be "borrowed" from compound meter, since it sounds exactly the same as the normal division of three in compound meter.

Section 2. Duplet division of dotted note values.

In example 14.18, *a, b,* and *c* sound identical when performed at the same tempo. The duplet in compound meter could be said to be "borrowed" from simple meter, since it sounds exactly the same as the normal division of two in simple meter.

At *c,* the duplet notation as two dotted eighth notes is mathematically accurate. Each dotted eighth note is equivalent to three sixteenth notes, exactly one-half of the six sixteenth notes in the beat. This notation is less commonly used.

Section 3. Two-part drills.

The goal of these drills is the ability to perform simple and compound rhythmic units simultaneously, a common situation for keyboard players, as well as for any musician performing a part in one meter while another meter is sounding.

In examples 14.29 and 14.30 (simple meter signature), think simple and then compound as you alternate hands. Repeat until the transition from one to the other is easily accomplished, then go past the repeat bar, performing simple and compound units simultaneously.

In examples 14.31 and 14.32 (compound meter signature), follow the same procedure, alternating your thinking and performing, first in compound meter and then in simple meter, followed by simultaneous performance of the two meters.

SIGHT SINGING

Section 4. Triplet division of undotted note values.

14.39 Langsam Yiddish, *Die drai Nejtorns*

14.40 Slowly California

14.41 Slowly Hebrew, *Etz Hayim Hi*

14.42 Langsam Portugal

14.43 Andante   Portugal

14.44 Allegro   Spain

14.45

Slowly   Spiritual, United States

14.46

Slowly   Hebrew, *Sahaki*

14.47

Moderato   Schubert, *Am Strome*, Op. 8, No. 4

14.48

Moderato   Costa Rica

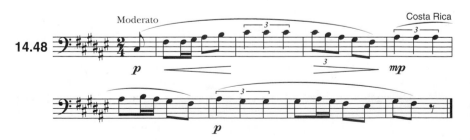

14.52

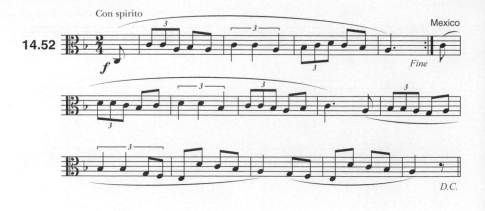

Con spirito

Mexico

f

Fine

D.C.

14.53

Andante con moto

Venezuela

Section 5. Duplet division of dotted note values.

14.54

Moderato

Utah

mf

cresc.

14.55

Allegro

Spain

14.56

Assez animé

France

14.57

Moderato

Pennsylvania

14.58

14.59

14.60

14.61 Lento ... Spain

14.62 Modéré et gracieux ... France

14.63 Herzlich ... Brückler (1845–1871), *Als ich zum erstenmal dich sah*

14.64

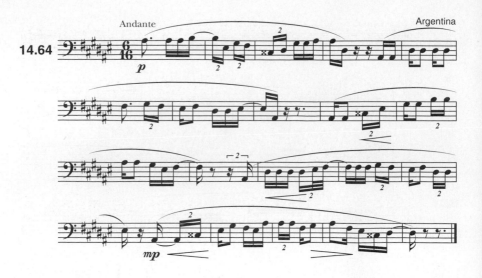

Section 6. Duets.

14.65

14.66

Section 7. Structured improvisation.

➤➤ Elaborate the basic framework below with stepwise motion, placing each given note on the downbeat. You may use any rhythmic pattern from previous chapters, but try to include at least two triplet figures.

➤➤ Elaborate the harmony indicated below each bracket using passing tones and chordal skips similar to the first measure (but not necessarily maintaining the same contour in each measure). Include at least one triplet per measure.

➤➤ By maintaining coherent melodies in different registers, exercise 14.70 implies two distinct voices. The effect is essentially like a duet, but with only one performer. Complete the melody by elaborating the two-voice outline provided, similar to the way in which the first measure elaborates B♭–G (shown above the staff). Leap between the two implied voices at least once in each measure, and try to include several triplets.

MELODY

Chromaticism (I)
Chromatic Embellishing Tones;
Tonicizing the Dominant;
Modulation to the Key of the
Dominant or the Relative Major

Section 1. Chromatic notes in the context of stepwise motion.

Chromatic notes are those that are not members of the scale of the key in which the music sounds. Examples: In C major, F is diatonic, F♯ is chromatic; in D major, F♯ is diatonic, F𝄪 is chromatic; in B♭ major, A♭ is diatonic, A is chromatic. In its usual stepwise resolution, a raised chromatic note moves up a half step to the next diatonic note, and a lowered chromatic note moves down a half step to the next diatonic note. The opening examples of this chapter illustrate representative embellishing usages: as a neighboring tone (melody 15.1) or a passing tone (melodies 15.6). Different solmization systems identify chromatic notes differently. A variety of popular approaches is explained in Appendix B.

Different solmization systems identify chromatic notes differently. A variety of popular approaches is explained in Appendix B.

15.6

Andante

Schubert, *Ecossaisen* No. 3

pp

mp

15.7

Geschwind

F. Freystädtler, *Mahonet der Zweite* (1795)

15.8

Schubert, *German Dance*, D. 973, No. 3

15.9

Allegro   Russia

15.10

Andante cantabile   Schumann, Piano Quartet, Op. 47

rit.

15.11

Allegro e marcato   Russia

15.12

Presto ma non troppo   Chopin, Mazurka, Op. 7, No. 4

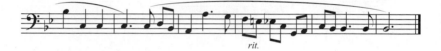

15.13 Andante moderato   Mozart, Mass in C Minor, K. 427

Section 2. Chromatic notes approached or left by leap.

Chromatic notes are sometimes approached by leap or, less often, left by leap; see melody 15.14 (which begins with double neighbors, also known as changing tones) and melody 15.16 (which includes some chromatic appoggiaturas). Chromatic appoggiaturas may produce augmented or diminished intervals with the notes that precede them. One way to negotiate a difficult leap to a chromatic note is to think of the note that follows the chromatic note, and then relate this note back to the chromatic note. For example, in melody 15.18, you will see an appoggiatura E♯ resolving to F♯ in D major. Think about the F♯ that continues the stepwise descent from B starting in measure 3, then lead into that F♯ goal from a half step below — the E♯ appoggiatura. Alternatively, you might notice that the E♯ in melody 15.18 is part of a longer chromatic ascent from the D that begins in measure 1. Contextualizing chromatic notes so that we can understand their relationships to diatonic notes makes them easier to sing.

15.14 Moderato   Costa Rica

15.15 Animated — Brahms, *Vergebliches Ständchen*, Op. 84, No. 4

15.16 Moderato con moto

15.17 Vivace — Haydn, String Quartet, Op. 74, No. 1

15.18 Allegretto — Joseph Steffan (1726–1797), *Gold'ne Freiheit*

15.19 Allegro assai — Haydn, *Farewell Symphony*

15.20 Andante con moto   Bizet, "O cruelle infidelle" from *La jolie fille de Perth*

On what chromatically altered scale degree does this melody begin?

15.21   Mozart, Serenade, K. 239

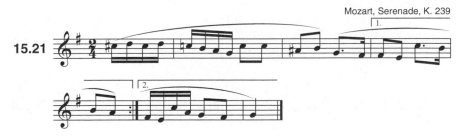

15.22 Poco allegretto   Beethoven, Piano Sonata, Op. 7

15.23

Section 3. Tonicization of V in major keys.

The presence of the raised tone #$\hat{4}$ in a melody often indicates the use of a secondary dominant harmony. In its frequent appearance at a cadence point, it implies either a tonicized half cadence V/V→V (C major: D F# A→G B D) or a modulation to the dominant (C major: F# is the leading tone in G major).

On paper, such a progression *looks* like a modulation, with the pivot chord I = IV, but it often *sounds* like a half cadence in the original key. Choosing an analysis is not always easy, as the perception of reaching or not reaching a new key will differ from person to person. When hearing or performing such a progression, it helps to ask yourself, "Could the composition stop at this point or must it continue?" If the music must continue, considering the progression as a half cadence is often the better choice.

The melodies in this section illustrate cadences on the dominant, all of which may be interpreted as tonicizations. At a modulation, people who sing with movable-*do* solfège or scale-degree numbers typically shift their syllables so that the local tonic is called *do* or $\hat{1}$ (see sections 4 and 5 of this chapter), but no such shift is needed at a tonicization. Thus, the melodies in this section may be performed with no change in solmization. However, many of these melodies are open to interpretation. If you perceive a change of tonic (and you use a movable solmization system), adjusting your solmization to reflect that change is quite appropriate.

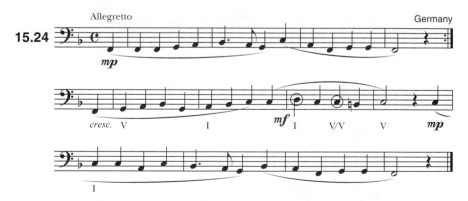

15.24

Notice that it is possible to tonicize V without including any accidentals in the melody.

15.28 With breadth and vigor — Byrd, *Make Ye Joy to God*

15.29 Largo — Haydn, Symphony No. 88

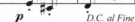

D.C. al Fine

15.30 Allegro — Mozart, *Sehnsucht nach dem Frühlinge*, K. 596

15.31

Allegro   Scotland

mf

f

1.

2.

mf

15.32

Ziemlich lebhaft   Schubert, *Der Musensohn*

15.33

Langsam   Schubert, *Du bist die Ruh*

pp

15.34

Jolly   England

f   *p*

15.35

Menuetto   Beethoven, Piano Sonata, Op. 22

p

15.36

Mässig bewegt   Germany

mf

f–p

15.37

Schubert, Minuet, D. 41, No. 18

15.38 Allegretto   Handel, *Xerxes*

15.39 Moderato   Schubert, *Mit dem grünen Lautenbande*

15.40 Schumann, *Der Kartenlegerin*, Op. 31, No. 2

Allegro

15.41 Arriaga, String Quartet No. 2 (1822)

Andante

15.42 Schumann, *Marienwürmchen*, Op. 79, No. 14

Nicht schnell

15.43

Section 4. Tonicization of III and modulation to the relative major from minor keys.

In minor keys, it is not unusual to touch on the relative major through a tonicization of the III chord or a modulation to the key of III. People who sing using scale-degree numbers or *do*-based minor often find that shifting their solmization makes it easier to perform such passages. The tonicization in melodies 15.44 and 15.45 is weak and may not warrant any adjustment. However, melody 15.46 will probably be made easier by shifting to the relative major at the first asterisk ($\hat{6} = \hat{4}$, or *le* = *fa*) and shifting back again at the second asterisk. (People who sing using *la*-based minor or a fixed system will maintain the same solmization throughout.)

15.44

15.45

15.46

Lightly   Yiddish, *Ver Zhe Klapt Dort in Mayn Tir?*

15.47

Adagio   Slovakia

15.48

Langsam   Yiddish, *Achtzig Er un Siebetzig Sie*

15.49

Adagio   Germany (Brahms)

15.50 Andante con moto — Schubert, *Rosamunde*, Op. 26

15.51 Con moto — Karg-Elert, Etude, Op. 41, No. 18

15.52 Andante — Anonymous, *A Catch Upon Port Wine*

15.53 Moderato — Yiddish, *Sog Nit Kejnmol*

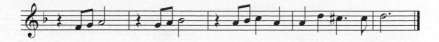

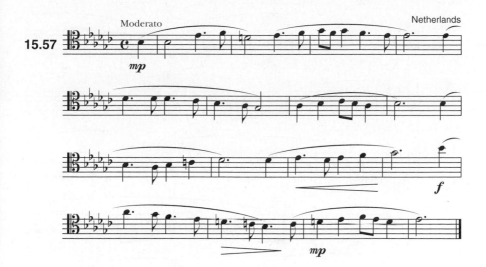

15.57 Moderato — Netherlands

mp

f

mp

15.58 Allegro — Yiddish, *Nochumke, main Suhn*

mf

15.59 Allegro — Fauré, *Fleur Jetée*, Op. 39, No. 2

f

mf

f

Langsam   Schubert, *Wasserflut*, Op. 89, No. 6

15.60

Section 5. Modulation to the dominant from major and minor keys.

It is very common for music to modulate to the key of its dominant. For a work in C major, this means changing to G major; for a work in C minor, this means changing to G minor (not G major, which has fewer notes in common with C minor). As discussed in section 3 of this chapter, the distinction between a tonicization and a modulation is not always clear, but the melodies in this section are likely to be interpreted as modulating. People who use a moveable solmization system should shift their syllables to reflect a perceived change of tonic. A suggested location for such a shift is marked with an asterisk in melody 15.61.

Handel, *Julius Caesar*

15.61

15.62

Adagio   Germany

15.63

Trio (menuetto)   Mozart, Serenade, K. 100

15.64

Frisch   Schubert, *Die Alpenjäger*, Op. 13, No. 3

15.65

Anonymous, from *Noten-Büchlein vor Anna Magdalena Bach*

15.66

Ländler

Austria

15.67

Allegro

Yiddish, *Dennoch frejlech*

15.68

Moderato

France

15.69

15.70

15.71

Schubert, Minuet, D. 380, No. 1

15.75

Mit innigkeit

Germany

15.76

Schubert, Minuet, D. 41

15.77

15.78 Allegro — Beethoven, *Maigesang*, Op. 52, No. 4

15.79 Andante — Purcell, *The Fairy Queen*

15.80 Allegretto — Netherlands

15.81 Reichardt, *Der König von Thule*

Langsam

15.82 Mozart, *Das Kinderspiel*, K. 598

Munter

15.83 Schumann, *Kinder Sonata*, Op. 118a, No. 1

Allegro

258

Schumann, Piano Quintet, Op. 44

15.87

Section 6. Duets.

15.88 Allegretto   Germany

15.89 Moderato   Germany

15.90

Allegro

Mozart, *The Magic Flute*, K. 620

15.91

Allegro

Bach, Cantata No. 197

15.92

Allegretto

Mozart, String Quartet, K. 575

Section 7. Structured improvisation.

➤➤ A melodic outline for two phrases is provided below. Elaborate the given notes (all of which fall on the beat) with the opening measure's neighbor-note figure, using chromatic inflection whenever possible.

➤➤ A melodic outline for one phrase is provided below. Using entirely stepwise motion and any combination of ♪ and ♩ that fits the meter, connect these notes (all of which fall on the beat) so that they form a melody. Include some chromatic neighboring and/or passing tones.

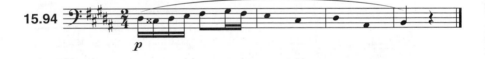

➤➤ Complete the melody by outlining the harmonies indicated below each bracket. You may use notes outside the specified chords on metrically weak beats, provided that you approach and resolve them by step. A rhythmic pattern has been suggested in several locations.

16

MELODY

Chromaticism (II)
Tonicization of Any Diatonic Triad;
Modulation to Any Closely Related Key

Section 1. Tonicization of any diatonic triad; modulation only to the dominant or relative major key.

The first section of this chapter freely mixes the tonicizations and modulations introduced in Chapter 13. Thus, it will be especially important to examine each melody closely and assess the overall tonal structure before sight singing. This section also includes secondary dominant harmonies other than V/V. For example, melody 16.2 includes the progression V/ii→ii in measures 15–16 (A major: F♯ A♯ C♯ → B D F♯). It is possible to tonicize any major or minor (but not diminished) triad.

16.5

Germany (Brahms)

p

Fine

D.C. al Fine

16.6

Adagio

Liadov, Sarabande

p

cresc.   *f*

16.7

Etwas lebhaft

Schubert, *Die Forelle*

p

16.8

Largo

Nörmiger, *Tablaturbuch* (1598)

mp

Fine   *cresc.*

f   *D.C. al Fine*

16.9

Allegro

16.10

Andantino

Brazil

16.11

Canon for 3 voices

Beethoven

16.15

16.16

16.19 Beethoven, String Quartet, Op. 18, No. 5

16.20 Loillet, Sonata for Flute, Op. 2, No. 3

16.21 Mozart, Clarinet Quintet, K. 581

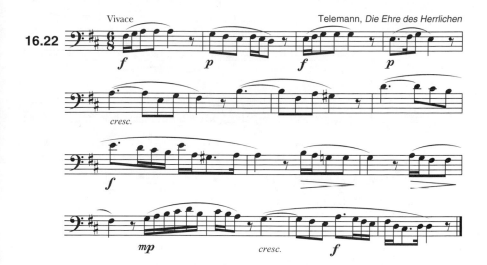

16.22 Vivace — Telemann, *Die Ehre des Herrlichen*

16.23 Allegro — Beethoven, String Quartet, Op. 18, No. 4

16.24 Schumann, *Du Ring am meinem Finger,* Op. 42, No. 4

16.25 Sarabande — Purcell, Suite V

16.26 Siciliano — Purcell, Suite II

16.27

Allegro   Brazil

mf

f

16.28

Marcia   Berlin, "I've Got My Captain Working for Me Now"

16.34 Schumann, *Der Zeisig*, Op. 104, No. 4

16.35 Haydn, String Quartet, Op. 55, No. 2

16.36 Görner, *Die vorliebte Verz*

16.37

Andante

16.38

Andante   Mozart, *La Clemenza di Tito*, K. 621

16.39

Andante con moto   Haydn, String Quartet, Op. 71, No. 3

16.40

Allegro frenetico

Berlioz, "Chanson à boire" from *Irlande*, Op. 2

16.41

Presto

Haydn, Piano Sonata (1776)

16.42

Zart, heimlich

Brahms, *Geliebter, wo zaudert*, Op. 33, No. 13

16.43 Moderato — Irving Berlin, "A Pretty Girl Is Like A Melody"

16.44 Zart — Brahms, *Wie Melodien zieht es mir*, Op. 105, No. 1

p sempre dolce

Section 2. Modulation to any closely related key.

In contrast to the nebulous quality of modulatory or secondary dominant progressions to the dominant, a modulation to any other key is usually more convincing, since its cadence usually has little or no inclination to return immediately to the original key. Of all the possible modulations to closely related keys,[1] those to the dominant, the relative major, and the relative minor are the most common.

[1]When the signatures of two keys are the same, or differ by not more than one sharp or one flat, the keys are considered closely related. Examples:

from C major to D minor (1♭)	from C minor to E♭ major (3♭)
to E minor (1♯)	to F minor (4♭)
to F major (1♭)	to G minor (2♭)
to G major (1♯)	to A♭ major (4♭)
to A minor (0♯ or ♭)	to B♭ major (2♭)

16.48

Allegro moderato

Purcell, *Dido and Aeneas*

Fine *mp*

cresc.

D.S. al Fine

16.49

Langsam

Schubert, *Das Zügenlächlein*

cresc.

f

16.54 Allegro — Mozart, String Quintet, K. 406

16.55 Allegretto — Italy

16.60

Andantino grazioso

Franz, *Liebchen ist da!*, Op. 5, No. 2

16.61

Allegro

Franz, *Genesung*

16.62

Poco meno mosso

Liadov, Arabesque, Op. 4

16.63

Allegro molto

Beethoven, String Quartet, Op. 18, No. 2

16.64

Andantino

Germany

16.65

Gavotte

Lully, *Le marriage forcé*

16.69

Bach, Mass in B Minor, *Qui sedes*, BWV 232

16.70

Mozart, Sonata for Piano and Violin, K. 402

Section 3. Duets.

Included are examples of both secondary dominant progressions and modulations to closely related keys.

16.74 (Allegro) Handel, Sonata for Flute and Continuo

16.75

16.76

H. Albert, *Cras serum est vivere* (1638)

16.77

16.78   Langsam   Cornelius, *Lied des Narren*

Section 4. Structured improvisation.

➤➤ Complete the partial melody below as indicated. Notice that measure 2 will modulate to the relative major, then measure 3 will gradually return to the original minor key. (Helpful hint: an A♯ in measure 3 will make the return to the relative minor more convincing.)

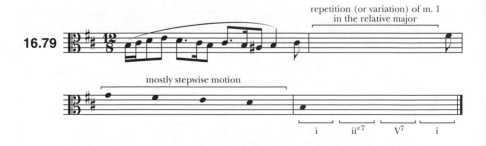

16.79

repetition (or variation) of m. 1
in the relative major

mostly stepwise motion

i   ii^{ø7}   V⁷   i

➤➤ Complete the given melody, following the harmonies indicated below the brackets. You may simply arpeggiate the chords, or you may elaborate them with passing tones and neighboring tones. Restrict yourself to rhythmic values no shorter than an eighth note.

16.80

➤➤ Improvise two phrases according to the outline below. The notes provided should fall on the beat, and your melody should elaborate the harmonies shown below the brackets. Notice that the second phrase modulates to the key of the dominant; the perfect authentic cadence indicated at the end is in the new key.

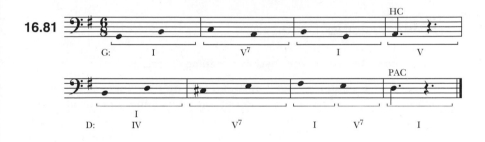

16.81

17

RHYTHM AND MELODY

Changing Meter Signatures;
The Hemiola;
Less Common Meter Signatures

RHYTHMIC READING

Section I. Definitions and rhythmic reading exercises.

Changing meters (melodies in Section 2). One or more changes of meter may occur within a composition. Most commonly, the changes occur all within simple meter or all within compound meter, the denominators of the signatures remaining constant. Consequently, the duration of the beat is the same in each meter. A new meter signature is placed at the point of each change.

When the change is from simple meter to compound meter, or the reverse, there are two distinct possibilities:

1. The divisions of the two meters are of equal duration (often indicated in the score by a symbol such as ♪ = ♪ at the point of the change). Example 17.3 shows that the eighth note of $\frac{6}{8}$ is equal in value to the eighth note of $\frac{2}{4}$. When this particular type of meter change occurs, the tempo of the beat will change while the tempo of the divisions remains constant.

2. When a symbol such as ♩ = ♩. appears, the durations of the two note values are equal. In example 17.7a, the quarter note of 2/4 is equal in duration to the dotted quarter note of 6/8. Example 17.7b shows how the same rhythmic sound can be notated with the use of triplets. When this particular type of meter change occurs, the tempo of the beat will remain constant while the tempo of the divisions will change.

A double meter signature combines the two signatures to be used during the composition. After the double signature $\frac{3}{4}\frac{2}{4}$, for example, each measure will be either $\frac{3}{4}$ or $\frac{2}{4}$ without further indication. Such a signature often indicates a regular alternation between the two meters—$\frac{3}{4}\frac{2}{4}\frac{3}{4}\frac{2}{4}$—or a pattern of successive meters, such as $\frac{3}{4}\frac{3}{4}\frac{2}{4}\frac{3}{4}\frac{3}{4}\frac{2}{4}$. Triple signatures such as $\frac{4}{4}\frac{2}{4}\frac{3}{4}$ are possible but rare.

The *hemiola* (melodies in Section 3) is a change of grouping that suggests a change of meter without the use of a changing meter signature. In this device, two successive groups of three beats (or three divisions) create the aural impression of three groups of two beats (or two divisions)—for instance, ♩♩ ♩♩ ♩♩ becomes ♩♩ ♩♩ ♩♩.

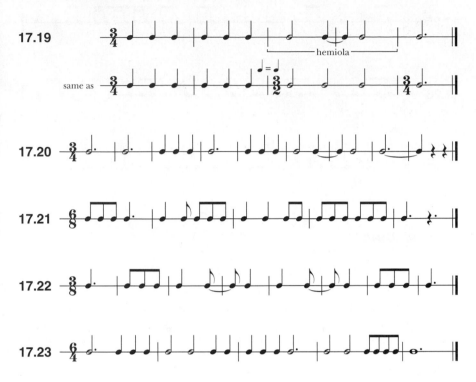

Meters of 5 and 7 (melodies in Section 4). These meter signatures usually sound like two alternating meters, such as $\frac{5}{4} = \frac{3}{4}\frac{2}{4}$ or $\frac{2}{4}\frac{3}{4}$, or $\frac{7}{8} = \frac{4}{8}\frac{3}{8}$ or $\frac{3}{8}\frac{4}{8}$. The beat groupings are usually reflected by the notation, such as ♩♩♩ ♩♩ for 3 + 2. The 3 + 4 grouping of melody 17.70 is indicated by a dotted bar line within each measure. A constant alternation can be indicated by a signature such as $\frac{3+2}{4}$. Other meter signatures are uncommon in music before the twentieth century; they must be interpreted on an individual basis.

The Conductor's Beats: five and seven beats per measure

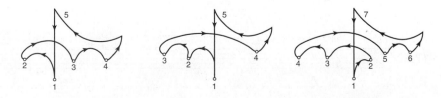

SIGHT SINGING

Section 2. Changing meter signatures.

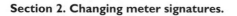

17.31  Largo — France

p

Fine *mf* D.C. al Fine

17.32  Andante — France

p

mf

sf *p*

17.33  Andante grazioso — Brahms, Piano Trio, Op. 101

p dolce

1.   2.

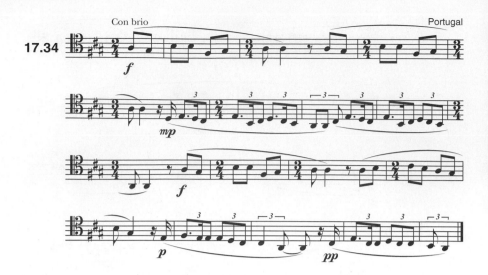

17.34 Con brio ... Portugal

17.35 Allegro ... France

17.36 Allegro ... Jamaica

17.37 Andante cantabile ... Tchaikovsky, *Sleeping Beauty*

17.38 Brahms, *Es rauschet das Wasser*, Op. 28, No. 3

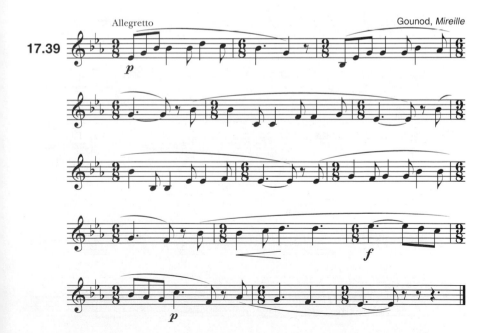

17.39 Gounod, *Mireille*

Section 3. The hemiola.

Example 17.43 demonstrates the "classic" sound and notation for the hemiola: one or more three-beat groupings followed by a group of three two-beat groupings. Their notation and placement in context vary widely, as can be seen in these melodies, but each expresses a 3–2 or 2–3 relationship.

17.44. In $\frac{6}{8}$: two groups of three eighth notes are followed by a group of three quarter notes within one measure of $\frac{3}{4}$.

17.45. The 3–2 relationship reversed: three groups of two eighth notes are followed by two groups of three eighth notes (2–3).

17.46. There are two successive groups of hemiolas.

17.47. The cadence usually expected for $\frac{3}{4}$, measures 7–8, is preceded by three successive groups of two.

The hemiola was used frequently in the seventeenth and eighteenth centuries but saw declining interest in the ninteenth century, except in the music of Johannes Brahms and Hugo Wolf. The twentieth century saw its increased usage along with similar devices that expressed the revival of rhythmic freedom.

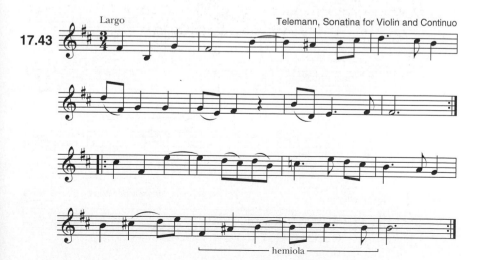

17.44

Spiritoso

Bohemia

17.45

Lively

Venezuela

17.46

Lento

Pergolesi, *Piangerò tanto*

17.47

Im Ländler tempo

Brahms, *Liebeslieder Walzer*, Op. 52, No. 2

17.48 Allegro molto   Mexico

17.49 Allegro   Bach, Sonata No. 3 for Flute and Clavier

17.50

C minor: V⁷/iv

17.51

Allegro

Bach, *Brandenburg Concerto No. 4*

17.52

Allegro molto

Spain

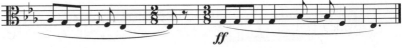

308

Section 4. Meters of 5 and 7, and other meters.

17.57

Spain

17.58

Venezuela

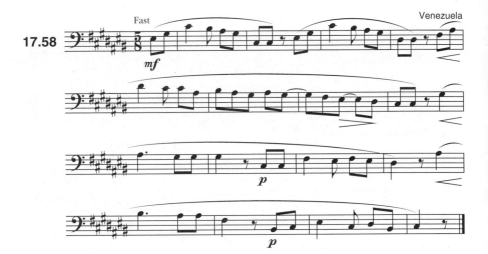

17.59

Mexico

17.64

Allegretto   Bernstein, *Candide*, "The Ballad of Eldorado"

pp simply and gracefully

mp

cresc.

mf   *p* dim.

17.65

Allegro spiritoso (3 + 4)   Greece

f

1.   2.

1.   2.

17.66

Molto moderato (4 + 3)   Scotland

mp

17.67

Allegro moderato   Croatia

f

1.   2.

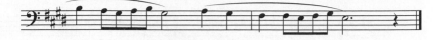

17.68 Moderato — Albania

mf

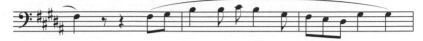

p

17.69 Allegro non troppo — Mexico

mf

17.70 Molto moderato — Elgar, *Caractacus*

p

17.71   Molto moderato e pesante   Borodin, *Song of the Dark Forest*

17.72   Andante   Nova Scotia

17.73   Presto   Mexico

17.74 Pas vite — France

17.75 Maestoso — Rimsky-Korsakov, *The Snow Maiden*

17.76 Andantino (♩ = 84) — Mussorgsky, *Boris Godunov*

17.77

Section 5. Structured improvisation.

➤➤ Continue this melody using mostly stepwise motion and the leap of a third between the last two notes of every measure. Try to sustain the rhythm of constant eighth notes throughout. (You may prefer to deviate from established patterns in the last measure, however.)

17.78

➤➤ Elaborate the harmony indicated below each bracket using passing tones and chordal skips similar to the first measure. Although you should incorporate similar features in order to create the sense of a unified phrase, you need not adhere to a single repeating contour or rhythm. Notice that the meter consistently alternates between $\frac{3}{4}$ and $\frac{2}{4}$.

17.79

➤➤ Improvise a consequent phrase to answer the antecedent phrase provided below. Try to begin the second phrase with contrasting material, but be careful to maintain the established hemiola pattern throughout. End with a very strong cadential gesture so that the final cadence sounds more conclusive than the cadence in measure 4.

17.80

RHYTHM AND MELODY

Further Subdivision of the Beat;
Notation in Slow Tempi

The use of note values smaller than the divisions presented in previous chapters is relatively uncommon. Divisions smaller than those shown below are possible, but they are rarely used.

1. The beat note is divided into eight parts in simple meters and into twelve parts in compound meters. In signatures with other denominators, the beat note may be similarly divided.

For these divisions to be performed using the usual note value for one beat (as indicated by the meter signature), the tempo must be moderate to slow, but not as slow as described below.

2. The division of the beat (as indicated by the meter signature) is used as the beat-note value. When the tempo of a composition is very slow, the meter signature often does not actually express the number of beats in the measure. In a very slow $\frac{2}{4}$ measure, for example, there may actually be four beats, the eighth note receiving one beat. Similarly, in a very slow tempo, the numerator

of the meter signature for a compound meter may actually indicate the number of beats in the measure. Consequently, in a slow §, instead of two ♩. beats in one measure, there might be six ♪ beats in one measure.

It is sometimes difficult to ascertain when to use the beat division as the actual beat note. Beginning with Beethoven, who first made use of the metronome, composers at times include a metronome marking for the beat division, as in melody 18.22, where the eighth note receives the beat in ¾ time, and in melody 18.23, where the subdivision, a sixteenth note, is designated as the beat in ¾ time.

When no marking is supplied by the composer, an editorial marking in parentheses is sometimes included in the score, as in melody 18.26. Such a marking is based on the composer's tempo indication or determined through knowledge of the composer's style and of historical performance precedents. When not indicated, the beat-note value must be similarly determined by the performer. But there will always be borderline cases where a slight difference in opinion can result in a different choice of beat-note value.

Section I. Rhythmic reading.

Read each example, using these metronome markings:

18.1–18.6: M.M. ♩ = 50
18.7–18.8: M.M. ♩ = 50
18.9–18.11: M.M. ♪ = 44

Read each example again, using these metronome markings:

18.1–18.6: M.M. ♪ = 76
18.7–18.8: M.M. ♩ = 76
18.9–18.11: M.M. ♪ = 86

Read these examples using the metronome marking M.M. ♪ = 72.

Section 2. Sight singing.

18.18   Con moto   France

18.19   Adagio   Haydn, Symphony No. 57

18.20   Moderato   Haydn, String Quartet, Op. 17, No. 5

18.21   Andante   Haydn, Symphony No. 90

18.22

Adagio cantabile ♪ = 72

Beethoven, String Quartet, Op. 18, No. 2

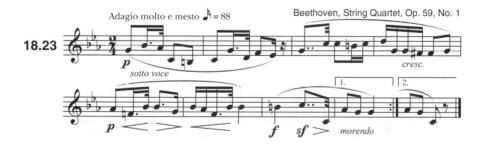

18.23

Adagio molto e mesto ♪ = 88

Beethoven, String Quartet, Op. 59, No. 1

18.24

Allegro

Verdi, *La Traviata*

18.25 Andante — Spohr, Double Quartet, Op. 87

18.26 Andante cantabile ($\flat$ = 80) — Donizetti, *Don Pasquale*

Handel, *Athalia*

18.31 Lentement   Rameau, *Hippolyte et Aricie*

18.32 Adagio, ma semplicemente   Haydn, Symphony No. 55

dolce

18.33

Allegretto

Auber, *Fra Diavolo*

Handel, *Serse*, Act II, Scene 12

18.34

Largo

Piccini, *La buona figliuola*

18.35

Sostenuto (♪ = 72)

Section 3. Structured improvisation.

➤➤ Maintaining a very slow tempo, construct a modulating phrase that follows the harmonic profile below. In general, elaboration such as passing tones and neighboring tones should fall on weak beats, while strong beats should emphasize chord tones. Try to cadence on the new tonic.

➤➤ Two common cadential bass formulas appear below. Elaborate each basic framework with neighboring tones, passing tones to other chord members, and occasional chordal skips. Some chords are open to interpretation (for instance, the B♭ in the first bass line might suggest iv or ii°⁶). Maintain a very slow tempo, and try to include some short note values such as ♪ and ♩.

MELODY

Chromaticism (III)

Additional Uses of Chromatic Tones;
Remote Modulation

Section 1. Chromatic tones in less common intervals.

The chromaticism in these melodies produces some infrequently used intervals. Examples include the diminished third (19.1), the augmented fourth (19.2), the augmented fifth (19.5), the augmented second (19.8), the diminished fourth (19.9), the minor ninth (19.10), and the diminished octave (19.15). Rather than focus on the difficult interval, however, it is generally best to think about how the chromatic note relates to nearby diatonic notes. For instance, in measures 1–2 of melody 19.1 it is helpful to hear the F♯ and A♭ as double neighbors around G, comparable to the double neighbors around E♭ one measure earlier.

Rossini, *La donna del lago*

19.1

19.2 Con moto — Mendelssohn, *O for the Wings of a Dove*

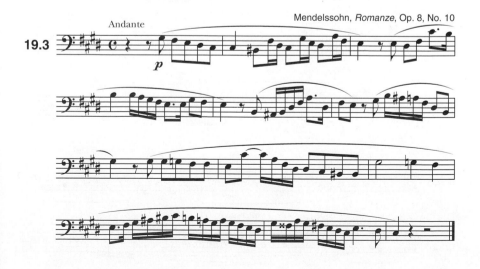

19.3 Andante — Mendelssohn, *Romanze*, Op. 8, No. 10

19.7

Slowly with much expression

Raymond Hubbell, *Poor Butterfly*

19.8

Vivace assai

Haydn, String Quartet, Op. 76, No. 2

19.9

Andante grazioso

Brahms, Clarinet Trio, Op. 114

19.10

Haydn, Symphony No. 52
Allegretto

19.11

Canon for 3 voices
Couperin

19.12

Andante
Handel, *Imineo*

19.13

Schumann, *Der schwere Abend*, Op. 90, No. 6

19.14

Schumann, String Quartet, Op. 40, No. 1

19.17

Allegro con spirito

Haydn, String Quartet, Op. 76, No. 1

19.18

Moderato

Beethoven, *Fidelio*, Op. 72

Im Ländler tempo

Brahms, *Liebeslieder Walzer*, Op. 52

19.19

Section 2. The Neapolitan sixth.

The distinctive chromatic melody tone $\flat\hat{2}$ usually implies the use of a major triad whose root lies a minor second above the tonic (in C major or C minor, D♭-F-A♭). In harmonic study, this chord is commonly known as the Neapolitan triad (the origin of the name is unknown) and may be represented by the symbol "♭II" or "N." The chord is typically found in first inversion (♭II⁶ or N⁶) and leads to the dominant, either directly, through a cadential $^6_4$ chord, or through vii°⁷/V.

In melodic writing, examples of the Neapolitan triad as three successive tones are not common. Nevertheless, example 19.20 shows the complete triad in both ascending and descending form; see also example 19.29. It is more common in melodic writing to use only the most characteristic tone, $\flat\hat{2}$, or to use two tones, one of which is $\flat\hat{2}$. In such cases, it is usually the harmonic context that identifies the triad's presence. In the second phrase of example 19.21, the downward movement of $\flat\hat{2}$ to $\sharp\hat{7}$ (C♮–A♯, a diminished third) indicates the probable harmony as ♭II⁶ resolving to V. Similarly, in example 19.26, measure 7, the interval E♭–C♯ suggests a progression from the Neapolitan to the dominant in D major. The preceding F♮ indicates a secondary dominant tonicizing the Neapolitan triad (B♭ D F→E♭ G B♭→A C♯ E).

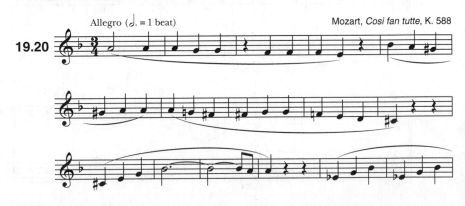

Allegro (♩. = 1 beat)

Mozart, *Così fan tutte*, K. 588

19.20

19.21 Allegretto   Italy

19.22 Canon for 3 voices   Caldara

19.23 Grazioso   Rimsky-Korsakov, *The Snow Maiden*

19.24 Allegro ben moderato — Meyerbeer, *L'Africaine*

19.25 Moderato — Sicily

19.26 Allegro — Mozart, Clarinet Quintet, K. 581

Mozart, String Quartet, K. 421

19.27

Beethoven, String Quartet, Op. 59, No. 2

Allegretto

19.28

pp

Schubert, *An Mignon*, Op. 19, No. 2

19.29

Schubert, *Der Müller und der Bach*

Mässig

19.30

Fine

D.C. al Fine

19.31 Andantino — Franz, *Mutter, o sing' mich zur Ruh'*

19.32 Ziemlich lebhaft — Schubert, *Des Sängers Fluchs*, Op. 139

Bach, Mass in B Minor, *Agnus Dei*, BWV 232

19.33

19.34 Allegro Grieg, *Des Dichters Herz,* Op. 5, No. 2

19.35 Presto Haydn, Symphony No. 52

Schumann, String Quartet, Op. 41, No. 3

19.36

Brahms, String Quintet, Op. 88

19.37

Section 3. Remote modulation.

A modulation to any key other than a closely related key is known as a *remote* (or *foreign*, or *distant*) modulation.

Schubert, *Spät schon, wenn schon längst*

19.38

19.39

Langsam

Schubert, *Wehmut*, Op. 22, No. 2

Schubert, *Jüngling am Bache*, Op. 87, No. 3

Berlioz, *The Damnation of Faust*

19.47

Mendelssohn, *Keine von der Erde schönen*, Op. post.

19.48 Andantino maestoso Rossini, *Le Chant des Titons*

19.49 Waltz tempo Schubert, Waltz, Op. 9, No. 14

19.50 Schumann, *Dein Angesicht*, Op. 127, No. 2

19.51 Borodin, *Song of the Dark Forest*

Section 4. Structured improvisation.

➤➤ Improvise a consequent phrase to answer the antecedent phrase provided below. Maintain a similar rhythmic profile, and try to incorporate several chromatic notes—particularly those borrowed from the parallel minor key.

➤➤ Elaborating the harmonic framework indicated below, improvise two four-measure phrases with an antecedent-consequent relationship.

➤➤ Improvise a modulating melody following the harmonic outline provided below. At first, you may want to restrict yourself to simple arpeggiations around the key change. Once the progression becomes more familiar, you will be able to elaborate all of the chords more consistently.

19.55

MELODY

The Diatonic Modes

The term *mode* refers to the arrangement of whole steps and half steps (or sometimes other intervals) to form a scale. In contrast to the present common use of major and minor modes, pre-seventeenth-century music was largely based on a system of six modes. These modes are also very common in folk music of the Western world. They were virtually neglected by composers of the seventeenth, eighteenth, and nineteenth centuries, but have again found favor in the twentieth and twenty-first centuries with composers of both serious and popular music.

The modes used in this chapter are those known variously as the *diatonic modes*, the *church modes*, the *ecclesiastical modes*, or the *medieval modes*.

Mode	White-note scale on keyboard[1]	Characteristic
Ionian	C	Same as major
Dorian	D	Similar to natural minor but with a raised sixth scale step
Phrygian	E	Similar to natural minor with a lowered second scale step
Lydian	F	Similar to major with a raised fourth scale step
Mixolydian	G	Similar to major with a lowered seventh scale step
Aeolian	A	Same as natural (pure) minor

[1]The mode on B, sometimes called *Locrian*, was not useful because of the interval of a tritone between tonic and dominant.

As an example, the Dorian mode can be realized by playing on the piano an ascending scale consisting of white keys only, starting on D. This results in a scale whose pattern of whole steps and half steps differs from the patterns of the well-known major and minor scales. This Dorian scale sounds somewhat like a minor scale but differs from D minor in that the sixth scale step is B♮ rather than B♭. The Dorian mode on D, therefore, has a signature of no sharps and no flats, although it is often found with a signature of one flat (D minor), with B♮ indicated throughout the composition.

Modes can be transposed to begin on any pitch or letter name. To transpose the Dorian mode to G, as in melody 20.6, note that the minor mode on G has two flats; raising the sixth scale step cancels the E♭, leaving one flat (B♭) in the scale. Usually the key signature uses those sharps or flats needed for its scale. In melody 20.20, the mode is Dorian on E; the key signature is two sharps, accommodating the C♯ found in this scale—E F♯ G A B C♯ D E. The signature of the parallel major or minor key may also be used. In melody 20.21, the mode is Mixolydian on A♭. The key signature is four flats, that of a major key on A♭. In the melody, a flat is added before each G($\hat{7}$)—A♭ B♭ C D♭ E♭ F G♭ A♭.

A modal melody can be found with one or more scale steps not used, making positive identification of the mode impossible. A melody with the tonic note D, using the pitches D E F G A–C D, could be Dorian with B missing or transposed Aeolian with B♭ missing (see melody 20.7).

Section I. Folk music.

20.3

Adagio   Iceland

20.4

Allegro   England

20.5

Moderato   Slovakia

20.6

Allegro   England

20.7

Slow   Newfoundland

20.8

Con moto   Massachusetts

20.9

Moderato   France

20.10 Allegro — Massachusetts

20.11 Andante — Scotland

20.12 Jovially — England

20.13

20.14

20.15

In number 20.16, $\hat{7}$ is raised when progressing directly or indirectly to the tonic note.

20.19 Allegro

Spain

20.20 Alla marcia

France

Section 2. Composed music.

In pre-seventeenth-century composed music, notes were sometimes altered by means of a device known as *musica ficta* ("feigned music"). Although the accidentals were not actually written, performers recognized that certain chromatic inflections were implied by the composer (either for aesthetic or practical reasons, such as avoiding augmented or diminished intervals). One particularly common example occurs at cadences: if $\hat{7}$ falls a whole step below $\hat{1}$, it is frequently raised a half step (comparable to the later practice of raising $\hat{7}$ in minor keys). In modern editions, an accidental is written *above* the note that was probably intended to be altered. Applying *musica ficta* affects the music's performance, but the mode is considered unchanged, as shown below.

20.27

Dufay, *Vergine bella*

20.28

Willaert, *Allons, allons gay*

20.29

20.30

Bartlet, *A Pretty Pretty Ducke*

20.31

Canon for 4 voices

Billings

20.32   Allegro vivace   Vaughan Williams, *The Wasps of Aristophanes*

20.33   Moderato   Ravel, *Chanson de la mariée*

20.34   Vincenzo Galilei, *Contrapuncti*

20.35

Lassus, *Crucifixus*

20.36

Josquin, *Missa ad Fugam*

20.37

20.38

20.39

20.40

Largo

Tallis, *Why Fumeth in Sight?* (1567)*

(Melody in Tenor)

*This melody was used by Ralph Vaughan Williams in his *Fantasia on a Theme of Thomas Tallis.*

Section 3. Structured improvisation.

➤➤ Using entirely stepwise motion, follow the suggested rhythm to create a G Dorian melody. Plan ahead so that you will end on G. (Note: You may wish to repeat this exercise in different modes.)

20.41

➤➤ Complete the partial melody below, including a balanced mixture of stepwise motion and leaps. A rhythm has been suggested. Be careful not to stray from the Mixolydian mode.

20.42

➤➤ Improvise a consequent phrase to answer the antecedent phrase provided below. Be careful to maintain the Aeolian mode, and focus on approaching the final D in a properly cadential manner.

20.43

21

RHYTHM AND MELODY

The Twentieth and Twenty-First Centuries

Presented in this chapter is a short introductory study of rhythmic and melodic writing in the twentieth century. During that time and into the twenty-first century, most composers of "serious music" have turned away from the precepts and methods of the preceding 300 years (Bach through Wagner), and instead have explored many new ways of expressing themselves in melody, harmony, and rhythm. The result has been a large catalogue of varying compositional styles, in contrast to the single "common practice" style featured in earlier chapters. The music examples that follow illustrate some of the new concepts that many such composers have developed in order to achieve basic characteristics differing from those of earlier periods.

Section 1. Meter and rhythm. Rhythmic reading.

Meter in music is no longer bound to a system of regular recurring accents and an equal number of beats in each measure. As an example, changing meters and less common meter signatures, similar to those seen in Chapter 17, are widely used. In any meter, bar lines no longer necessarily imply regularly recurring strong and weak beats, nor do meter signatures necessarily indicate the location of primary accents. Rhythmic patterns can be indicated by beaming of note values, phrase marks, and other notational devices. Bar lines, then, often function simply as a guide to the eye.

The rhythmic reading examples in this chapter illustrate some of the rhythmic and metrical practices that arose in the twentieth century and are not typical of common-practice music.

* No meter signature

21.10

21.11

Section 2. Extensions of the traditional tonal system.

Tonality did not by any means disappear at the end of the nineteenth century. However, many composers began to use traditional tonal features more flexibly. For instance, some music employs familiar diatonic collections without projecting a functional harmonic progression in the background (21.13), while other music provides fleeting glimpses of conventional harmony in the context of a rapidly shifting tonal center (21.18). Sometimes the melody seems to obscure the underlying harmony (21.22), suggesting a kind of hazy tonality where we can only barely recognize customary elements through the blurred sonic image.

To sight sing these melodies, first scan them for passages where the diatonic collection and/or the underlying harmony is clear. During these sections, it is appropriate to apply the solmization system you prefer for more traditional tonal music. When the collection or tonal center changes suddenly, focus on rapidly shifting the syllables. (This procedure will be familiar from navigating modulations in previous chapters.) When you encounter more ambiguous segments, employ a tonally neutral strategy such as intervals or letter names.

21.12

Scherzando, non rubato

Bartók, *Three Hungarian Folksongs from Csik*, Sz. 35a

21.13

With quiet grace

Copland, *Twelve Poems of Emily Dickinson*, "The Chariot"

21.14 Assez vif et triste — Ned Rorem, *Poemès pour la paix*, "Sonnet"

© *Copyright 1970 by Boosey & Hawkes, Inc. Reprinted by Permission.*

21.15 Allegro — Bartók, String Quartet No. 3

© *Copyright 1929 by Boosey & Hawkes, Inc. Copyright Renewed. Reprinted by Permission.*

Canon for 4 voices
Con slancio

Benjamin Britten, *Peter Grimes*

21.16

© *Copyright 1945 by Boosey & Hawkes Music Publishers Ltd. Reprinted by Permission.*

♩ = 60 (♩. = 45)

David Gompper, "Stork" from *The Animals*

21.17

Piu mosso

David Gompper, composer. Used by permission.

21.18

Allegretto   Jerome Kern, "Till the Clouds Roll By"

Kern, Jerome Wodehouse, P. G. New York 1917. T. B. Harms & Francis, Day & Hunter.

21.19

Vivace   Seymour Barab, *A Child's Garden of Verses*

mf

p

cresc.   *f*

© Copyright 1985 by Boosey & Hawkes, Inc. Reprinted by Permission.

21.20

♩ = 72   David Gompper, *Poetry for a Midsummer's Night,*
                       "Like Words, Like Music"

mp

David Gompper, composer. Used by permission.

379

Maurice Ravel, *Schéhérazade*

Allegro

Trés lent

Modéré

Rêveusement lent

Debussy, *En Sourdine*

Allegretto scherzando Claude Debussy, *Fêtes Galantes*, "Fantoches"

21.23

Prokofiev, *Visions fugitives*, Op. 22, No. 13

21.24 Allegretto

Deliberately ♩= 96 Jonathan Bailey Holland, *i thank you God most for this amazing*

21.25

Jonathan Bailey Holland, composer. Berklee College of Music, Vermont College of Fine Arts. Used by permission.

21.26

Dominick Argento, *Postcard from Morocco*

© *Copyright 1972 by Boosey & Hawkes, Inc. Reprinted by Permission.*

21.27

Britten, *Midsummer Night's Dream*

© *Copyright 1960 by Hawkes & Son (London) Ltd. Reprinted by Permission.*

21.28

Paul Hindemith, *Das Marienleben*, Op. 27

21.29 Andante pastorale   Sergei Prokofiev, *The Voice of Birds*, Op. 36, No. 2

21.30

21.31

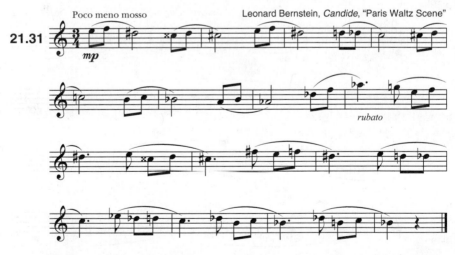

21.32

Lebhaft

Hindemith, *Mathis der Maler*

21.33

Allegretto

Dmitri Shostakovich, Symphony No. 10

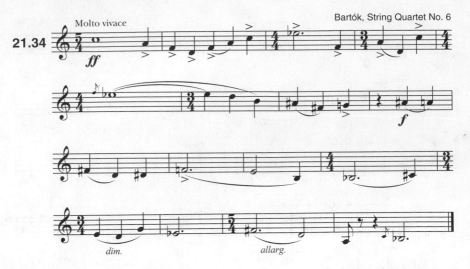

21.34

Molto vivace

Bartók, String Quartet No. 6

21.35

Rhythmique ♩ = 80

Arthur Honegger, *Pacific 231*

marcato

21.36

Allegro appassionato

Karol Szymanowski, "Werbung"

21.37

Meno mosso ♩ = ca. 88   Witold Lutosławski, "The Lime Tree in the Field"

pp

accelerando

Precipitando ♩. = ca. 60

poco f

rit.   Sostenuto

pp

Section 3. Symmetrical collections; the whole-tone and octatonic scales.

A substantial number of post-tonal compositions use special collections that are often described as *modes of limited transposition* or *transpositionally symmetrical scales*. These scales are constructed using a repeating interval pattern (such as M2–M2–M2–M2–M2 or M2–m2–M2–m2–M2–m2–M2–m2, as seen below); consequently, they produce an equivalent collection when transposed by some intervals (unlike the diatonic scale, which has twelve distinct transpositions). Two of the most important examples are shown here.

whole-tone scale (two transpositions)   octatonic scale (three transpositions)

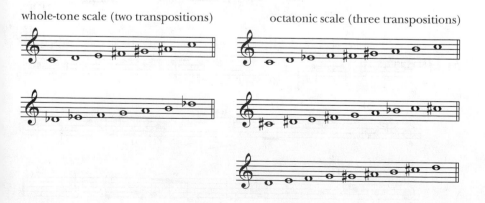

Just as identifying diatonic segments facilitates rapid and accurate sight singing of tonal and quasi-tonal literature, recognizing whole-tone and octatonic passages can lead to superior sight singing of certain post-tonal literature. To take advantage of this knowledge, however, a musician must first be able to sing the scales fluently.

The melodies in this section include at least one passage based on a mode of limited transposition. Before you begin sight singing, scan the melodies for passages involving a familiar collection (whole tone, octatonic, or diatonic). Actively concentrating on the distinctive sound and characteristic intervals of each scale will help to keep you oriented during these portions of the melody.

21.42 Andante ♩ = 108 Bartók, *Mikrokosmos*, No. 136, "Whole-Tone Scale"

p dolce

mp

© Copyright 1940 by Hawkes & Son (London) Ltd. Definitive corrected edition
© Copyright 1987 by Hawkes & Son (London) Ltd. Reprinted by Permission.

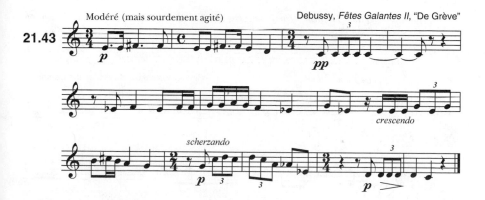

21.43 Modéré (mais sourdement agité) Debussy, *Fêtes Galantes II*, "De Grève"

p

pp

crescendo

scherzando

p

p

21.44 Modéré Debussy, *Fêtes Galantes II*, "Les Ingénus"

p

21.45

Très lent — Ravel, "Si Morne"

21.46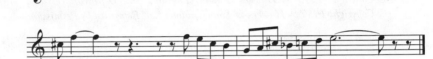

With intensity ♩. = 120 — Jonathan Bailey Holland, *Whitman's War*

Jonathan Bailey Holland, composer. Berklee College of Music, Vermont College of Fine Arts. Used by permission.

21.47

Andante ♩ = 96 — Rimsky-Korsakov, *Kashchey the Deathless*

21.48

Allegro molto ♩. = 104 — Lutosławski, "Bukoliki"

21.49

Andantino ♪ = 92

Stravinsky, Octet for Wind Instruments

ben cantabile **mp**

21.50

Allegro ♩ = 126–138

Bartók, *Two Pictures*, Sz. 46

21.51

David Gompper, Composer. Used by permission.

21.52

Rimsky-Korsakov, *Kashchey the Deathless*

Jonathan Bailey Holland, *Whitman's War*

21.53

Jonathan Bailey Holland, composer. Berklee College of Music, Vermont College of Fine Arts. Used by permission.

21.54

Whimsically ♩ = 92

Neil Anderson-Himmelspach, *Gonzo and the Velocipede*

Composed by Neil Anderson-Himmelspach. Used by permission.

21.55

Allegro cantabile
𝅗𝅥 = 60 ♩ = 120

Clifton Callender, "picking flowers" from *chansons innocents*

molto rit.

Composed by Clifton Callender. Used by permission.

Section 4. Freely post-tonal melodies; twelve-tone melodies.

The melodies in this section are freely chromatic, not oriented around conventional harmonic progressions or widely recognized scales (other than the chromatic scale). Sight singing them requires a flexible strategy: scan a melody for short segments that form a subset of a familiar collection, repeat a prominent motive, emphasize a specific interval, and so on. In order to take full advantage of your many skills, you may need to change your focus judiciously from moment to moment in response to the changing context.

21.56

Andante con moto ♩ = 72
child-like

Clifton Callender, "fourpaws" from *chansons innocents*

Composed by Clifton Callender. Used by permission.

Andante amoroso

Berg, *Lyrische Suite*

21.57

Alban Berg "Lyric Suite" © Copyright 1999 by UE Publishing Musikverlags GmbH/ UE 70017

Thomas Clark, *Isostrata*

21.58

Copyright 1979 by Subito Music Corp. All rights reserved. Reprinted by permission.

Largo (♩ = 38–40)
espressivo, ma semplice

Dallapiccola, *Frammenti di Saffo*

21.59

394

Sehr langsam   Schoenberg, "Schenk mir deinen goldenen Kamm," Op. 2

21.60

Used by permission of Belmont Music Publishers

Sehr fliessende Achtel   Anton Webern, *Gesang einer gefangenen Amsel*, Op. 14, No. 6

21.61

21.62

Mässig

Schoenberg, *Das Buch der hängenden Gärten*

p

rit.

Used by permission of Belmont Music Publishers.

21.63

♪ = 126

Stravinsky, *Rite of Spring*

*sempre **f** secco*

© *Copyright 1912, 1921 by Hawkes & Son (London) Ltd. Reprinted by Permission.*

Twelve-tone (or *dodecaphonic*) music derives its material from a twelve-tone *row* (or *series*), which is an ordering of all twelve distinct pitch classes.[1] Composers typically transform the original row using a variety of operations, including transposition, inversion, and retrograde.[2] If you examine the next several melodies, you will find that each one begins with a presentation of the complete chromatic collection. Melody 21.64 contains only one statement of the row, but in melodies 21.65, 21.66, and 21.67 you should be able to determine a specific relationship between the different row forms.

---

[1] The designation *serial music* is more general, referring to compositions based on an ordered series of any length. Although the ordering usually affects pitch, it could also involve durations, dynamics, orchestration, or any other musical parameter.

[2] Inversion and retrograde may be informally described as "upside down" and "backwards," respectively.

Notice that composers sometimes repeat notes within a row, and appearances of the row do not necessarily correspond with musical phrases. Can you guess the next few notes that follow the excerpt in melody 21.67?

21.64

21.65

Alan Theisen, composer. Used by permission.

21.66

Leggiero (like a quick, dark dream)
(♪. = 100)

Bernstein, *Songfest*,
"The Pennycandystore Beyond the El"

21.67

© Copyright by Amberson Holdings LLC. Copyright Renewed. Leonard Bernstein Music Publishing Company LLC, Publisher. International Copyright Secured. "The pennycandystore beyond the El." From A CONEY ISLAND OF THE MIND by Lawrence Ferlinghetti Copyright © 1958 by Lawrence Ferlinghetti. By permission New Directions Publishing Corporation. Reprinted by Permission.

Section 5. Duets.

Pesante

Schoenberg, Chamber Symphony, Op. 9

21.68

Adagio ♪ = 84

Jack Beeson, *Lizzie Borden*

21.69

Con moto ♩ = 110   Bartók, *Mikrokosmos*, No. 101, "Diminished Fifth"

21.70

21.71

21.72

Andante ♩ = 108 — Bartók, *Mikrokosmos*, No. 136, "Whole-Tone Scale"

21.73

Expressive — Glenn Caluda, *Four Introspections for Solo Guitar*

Sostenuto ♩ = ca. 100 — Lutosławski, "The Lime Tree in the Field"

Allegro — Merrill Ellis, Quintet for Oboe and Strings

♩ = 120

William P. Latham, *Epigrammata*

21.76

Section 6. Structured improvisation.

➤➤ The written portion of melody 21.78 revolves around one of the whole-tone collections. Complete it using only notes from the *other* whole-tone collection. Try to include at least one leap.

other whole-tone collection

➤➤ Continue the phrase, repeating the rhythmic pattern from measure 1 in measures 2 and 3. (You will probably want to change the rhythmic pattern in measure 4 to create a cadential effect.) In part *a*, restrict yourself to notes from the established whole-tone collection; in part *b*, maintain the octatonic collection.

21.79

➤➤ Improvise a phrase using only two intervals: the minor second and the major third. (Note: you may wish to repeat this exercise using other intervals.) An opening measure has been suggested.

21.80

APPENDIX A:
RHYTHM SOLMIZATION

There are innumerable rhythm solmization systems, but, despite their differences, most of them fall into four general categories:

- syllables emphasizing serial order
- syllables conveying metrical hierarchy
- syllables reflecting duration
- familiar words associated with specific rhythmic patterns

Many systems emphasize serial order—that is, where subdivisions fall within each beat and/or where beats fall within each measure. North American instrumentalists are often taught to count an entire measure of sixteenth notes in ²⁄₄ as *one-ee-and-ah, two-ee-and-ah* (often represented in print as *1-e-&-a 2-e-&-a*). Someone using the Takadimi system (developed by Richard Hoffman, William Pelto, and John W. White) would perform the same rhythm as *tah-kah-dee-mee, tah-kah-dee-mee* (written *ta-ka-di-mi*); notice that although subdivisions of beats are serialized in Takadimi, the beats themselves are not (i.e., all beats start with *ta*). Musicians who learn *1-e-&-a* for simple meters unfortunately are rarely taught to reflect the primary beat in compound meters; they tend to perform six eighth notes in ⁶⁄₈ as *one-two-three-four-five-six*, for example. Some count eighth notes in ⁶⁄₈ as *one-and-ah, two-and-ah*, but these same syllables unfortunately represent a significantly different rhythm in simple meters and can therefore lead to misunderstandings. Others borrow Allen I. McHose and Ruth N. Tibbs's preferable compound meter syllables, performing the same rhythm as *one-lah-lee, two-lah-lee* (*1-la-li 2-la-li*), appropriately communicating two beats per measure. Takadimi practitioners are invariably taught to express the primary beat divisions in compound meters as *tah-kee-dah, tah-kee-dah* (*ta-ki-da*), which also communicates two beats per measure.

A popular system conveying metrical hierarchy was developed by Edwin Gordon. Someone using this method will perform a note falling on any beat as *doo* (written *du*), while any notes that fall on the primary division of the beat are pronounced *day* (written *de*) in simple meters and *dah dee* (written *da di*) in compound meters. Notes on the weaker subdivision of the beat (e.g., the second and fourth sixteenth notes in $\frac{2}{4}$ or the second, fourth, and sixth sixteenth notes in $\frac{6}{8}$) are all pronounced *ta*. Thus, Gordon-inspired systems will use the same syllable to represent notes initiated on equally strong (or weak) portions of the beat, regardless of precisely where they fall within the measure. Notice the contrast with the Takadimi system, which provides a unique syllable to each subdivision within any given beat.

All of the systems mentioned thus far convey a note's starting point but not how long it lasts or how it is notated. For instance, two quarter notes in $\frac{2}{4}$, two dotted quarter notes in $\frac{6}{8}$, and two half notes in $\frac{3}{2}$ will all be performed the same way. A note of any length (half note, quarter note, eighth note, etc.) that falls on the downbeat will be performed the same way; however, that same note will be performed differently if it initiated off the beat (e.g., between the first and second beats of the measure). Some musicians prefer to use a very different solmization system that emphasizes a note's length rather than its onset relative to the underlying meter.

Perhaps the best-known approach reflecting duration is attributed to Zoltán Kodály (who adapted an existing system developed by Émile-Joseph Chevé). Although the specific syllables used vary slightly, the guiding principle is that notes that look the same generally receive the same syllable. For instance, a half note is pronounced *too*, a quarter note is pronounced *tah* (written *ta*), and eighth notes are pronounced *tee* (*ti*)—and this is true whether the meter signature is $\frac{3}{4}$ or $\frac{3}{2}$ or $\frac{6}{8}$, and regardless of where the note falls relative to the beat. In other words, duration-based systems reflect a note's appearance rather than its value in context (i.e., whether it represents a whole beat or a fraction of a beat, and whether it falls in a metrically strong or weak location). Some North Americans use an equivalent system that modifies our standard names for note values: for instance, a half note is *half*, a quarter note is *quart*, and an eighth note is *eighth* (or simply *eight*, because it is easier to say quickly); dotted notes may be conveyed by adding the syllable *dot*, although this will affect the rhythmic performance. For ease of pronunciation, duration-based systems often use pairs of syllables for short notes; for instance, four sixteenth notes might be performed *ti-ka-ti-ka, ti-ri-ti-ri,* or *six-teen-six-teen.*

Rhythmic speech cues are by their very nature idiosyncratic and tend to have some built-in amusement value, but they can also be extremely effective and have been favored by some prominent music educators, most notably Carl Orff. Specific words are carefully chosen not only for their syllable count but also for their accentuation and characteristic rhythm in natural speech. For instance, *watermelon* might convey four sixteenth notes in $\frac{2}{4}$, whereas *penny* might suggest a sixteenth note followed by a dotted eighth note.

For the sake of comparison and further clarification, two sample rhythms (one in simple meter and one in compound meter) are shown below with a variety of solmization systems.

a	1	3 &	1 e &	2 e & a	3	1———
b	ta	ta di	ta ka di	ta ka di mi	ta	ta———
c	du	du de	du ta de	du ta de ta	du	du———
d	ta	ti ti	ti ka ti	ti ka ti ka	ta	too———
e	quart	8 8	six- teen 8	six- teen six- teen	quart	half———
f	bear	ti- ger	pel- i- can	al- li- ga- tor	bear	lamb———

a	1	2 la li	1 ta la ta li ta	2 ta li	1	2 la	1
b	ta	ta ki da	ta va ki di da ma	ta di da	ta	ta ki	ta
c	du	du da di	du ta da ta di ta	du ta di	du	du da	du
d	tam	ti ti ti	ti ka ti ka ti ka	tim ka ti	tam	ti ta	toom
e	quart dot 8	8 8	six- teen six- teen six- teen	8 dot teen 8	quart dot 8	quart	half dot
f	bear	straw-ber- ry	pur-ple al- li- ga- tor	mas- to- don	bear	man-go	lamb

It is possible to combine aspects of different systems; for instance, one could easily say beat numbers rather than *du* in the Gordon system. Also, speech cues are often employed strategically to learn especially challenging rhythms, and they need not be maintained once a new pattern is mastered. Even musicians who ordinarily prefer a more systematic method often suggest performing quintuplets as *hippopotamus* or *university*.

So many rhythmic solmization systems exist that it is impossible to include them all in this appendix; furthermore, the systems represented have numerous minor variations. You may use an effective system that does not appear above. The important thing is to adopt an approach that helps you to understand and master new rhythms and enables you to perform them comfortably at a brisk tempo.

APPENDIX B:
PITCH SOLMIZATION

Different pitch solmization systems are categorized primarily by two independent features: whether a note receives the same name regardless of the music's key, and whether a note receives the same name regardless of whether it is preceded by an accidental. The former distinguishes fixed systems from movable systems; the latter distinguishes inflected systems from uninflected systems.

MOVABLE SYSTEMS

Movable systems promote relative pitch, fostering a general sense of tonal function and facilitating transposition skills. Movable-*do* solfège with *do*-based minor and scale-degree numbers are best suited to common-practice tonal music, while movable-*do* solfège with *la*-based minor is arguably more appropriate for modal music and some folk music.

1. **Movable-*do* solfège with *do*-based minor.** The tonic of any key is called *do* (pronounced *doe*). In a major key, the remaining notes of the ascending scale are *re* (pronounced *ray*), *mi* (pronounced *mee*), *fa*, *sol* (pronounced *so*), *la*, and *ti* (pronounced *tee*). Movable-*do* practitioners almost invariably convey chromatic inflection: the vowel for any raised note is changed to *i* (pronounced *ee*), and the vowel for most lowered notes is changed to *e* (pronounced *ay*), with the exception of *re*, which must be lowered to *ra*.[1] Thus, the ascending natural minor scale in this system is *do re me fa sol le te do*, emphasizing the consistent

---

[1]Although *e* is generally pronounced *ay*, some instructors advocate the vowel sound *eh* (e.g., *reh* rather than *ray* for the second scale degree) to facilitate good intonation on sustained notes.

function of scale degrees (such as the tonic) that are shared with the parallel major scale.

2. **Movable-*do* solfège with *la*-based minor.** This approach may be understood as privileging the connection between relative keys (such as C major and A minor) rather than parallel keys (such as C major and C minor). Although major keys are oriented around the tonic *do*, minor keys use *la* for the tonic. The ascending natural minor scale in this system is performed *la ti do re mi fa sol la*; using the inflections described above, the ascending melodic minor scale would be performed *la ti do re mi fi si la*. Musicians who regularly perform modal music often prefer this system, using solfège to help orient the naturally occurring half steps (*mi-fa* and *ti-do*). Notice that, in this approach, solmization is not intended to reflect any kind of tonal hierarchy: *do* is not necessarily the "home" note. (Music in the Dorian mode will likely end on *re*, for instance.)

3. **Scale-degree numbers.** In this system, notes in any major or minor key are named by their scale-degree numbers; any ascending major or minor scale is therefore $\hat{1}$ $\hat{2}$ $\hat{3}$ $\hat{4}$ $\hat{5}$ $\hat{6}$ $\hat{7}$ $\hat{1}$ (some people prefer to end with $\hat{8}$, which is also perfectly acceptable). The caret means "scale degree," and although ordinarily $\hat{2}$ would be read aloud as *scale-degree two*, for sight-singing purposes only the number itself is sung. To avoid altering rhythms, $\hat{7}$ is almost invariably performed as *sev* (rather than *seven*). Scale-degree numbers do not convey mode or chromatic inflection: *three* refers to the third scale degree in both major and minor keys, and most people identify both $\uparrow\hat{7}$ and $\downarrow\hat{7}$ as *sev*. However, some musicians who prefer an inflected system invent ways to express chromatic information using hand signals or changes in pronunciation (saying, for instance *shore* rather than *sharp four* for #$\hat{4}$ and *flee* rather than *flat three* for ♭$\hat{3}$).

FIXED SYSTEMS

Fixed systems promote absolute pitch (informally known as "perfect pitch") and may lead to superior clef reading. They can be used equally well for tonal, post-tonal, and modal music.

1. **Letter names.** North American musicians are quite familiar with this system, since we normally identify notes with letters, and these letter names do not vary from key to key. For instance, middle C remains *C* whether it is $\hat{1}$ in C major, $\hat{5}$ in F major, or $\uparrow\hat{6}$ in E♭ minor. Unfortunately, the application of flats and sharps also adds syllables in this system (e.g., *F-sharp* rather than *F*), and this interferes with rhythm when sight singing. Some musicians avoid this by treating the system as uninflected—referring, for instance, to D, D#, and D♭ simply as *D*. To convey chromatic inflections monosyllabically, others employ an adaptation of the German system: sharp notes start with their associated letter followed by *is* (pronounced *ees*), while flat notes start with their associated letter followed by *es* (pronounced *ess*). Using this system, for instance, G# is *Gis* (pronounced *geese*) and G♭ is *Ges* (pronounced *guess*). The exceptions to this pattern are A# (*ace*) and A♭ (*ice*).

2. **Fixed-*do* solfège.** Outside of North America, many musicians learn to identify notes with fixed solfège labels rather than letter names: the note that North Americans call C is *do*, D is *re*, and so on. Like letter names, fixed-*do* solfège does not vary according to key, so *do* does not necessarily refer to the tonic note; in F major, for example, the tonic is called *fa*. Although most fixed-*do* practitioners use an uninflected system (e.g., A, A♭, and A# are all *la*), chromatic inflections are easily conveyed using the system described earlier for movable-*do* solfège (e.g., A♭ is *le* and A# is *li*).

SOLMIZATION OF THE CHROMATIC SCALE

An ascending and descending chromatic scale in the context of F major is shown below with the corresponding solmization from a variety of systems.

Movable-*do* solfège:	do	di	re	ri	mi	fa	fi	sol	si	la	li	ti	do
Scale-degree numbers:	1̂	1̂	2̂	2̂	3̂	4̂	4̂	5̂	5̂	6̂	6̂	7̂	1̂
Inflected letter names:	F	Fis	G	Gis	A	Bes	B	C	Cis	D	Dis	E	F
Fixed-*do* solfège:	fa	fa	sol	sol	la	ti	ti	do	do	re	re	mi	fa

Fixed-*do* solfège:	fa	mi	mi	re	re	do	do	ti	la	la	sol	sol	fa
Inflected letter names:	F	E	Es	D	Des	C	Ces	Bes	A	Ice	G	Ges	F
Scale-degree numbers:	1̂	7̂	7̂	6̂	6̂	5̂	5̂	4̂	3̂	3̂	2̂	2̂	1̂
Movable-*do* solfège:	do	ti	te	la	le	sol	se	fa	mi	me	re	ra	do

SOLMIZATION OF A MELODIC FRAGMENT

For the sake of comparison and further clarification, a brief melodic fragment in G minor is shown below with the corresponding solmization from a variety of systems.

Movable-*do*, *do*-based minor:	do	te	le	sol	do	ti	do	re	me
Movable-*do*, *la*-based minor:	la	sol	fa	mi	la	si	la	ti	do
Scale-degree numbers:	1̂	7̂	6̂	5̂	1̂	7̂	1̂	2̂	3̂
Inflected letters:	G	F	Es	D	G	Fis	G	A	Bes
Uninflected fixed-*do* solfège:	sol	fa	mi	re	sol	fa	sol	la	ti

Recognizing the different strengths of movable and fixed solmization systems, some instructors prefer to adopt one of each (e.g., movable-*do* solfège and inflected letters).

APPENDIX C: MUSICAL TERMS

Most music commonly performed at the present time contains directions for performance, particularly in reference to tempo and dynamics. These markings were first added to music scores by a few Italian composers in the seventeenth century. As this procedure became more widespread, directions in Italian became standard in all languages. In the late nineteenth century, composers began using terms from their native languages, such as French, German, and English, though the older Italian terms continued to be commonly used.

This list presents a selection of terms frequently encountered in music, including all terms found in *Music for Sight Singing*. The language is Italian unless otherwise indicated: (F) = French, (G) = German, (L) = Latin.

a, à (F)   by
accelerando   getting faster
Achtel (G)   eighth note
adagietto   slightly faster than adagio
adagio   slow, leisurely
ad libitum (L)   at will (abbr. *ad lib*)
affetto   emotion, passion
affettuoso   very expressively
affretti   *hurried*
agitato   agitated
agité (F)   agitated
al   to

all', alla   to the, at the, in the, in the style of
allant (F)   stirring, bustling
allargando   growing broader, slowing down with fuller tone (abbr. *allarg.*)
allegretto   moderately fast; slower than allegro
allegro   lively, fast
all'ottava   perform an octave higher (when above the notes); perform an octave lower (when below the notes)
all'unisono   in unison

amoroso   amorous, loving
andante   moderately slow
andantino   slower than andante
animando   with growing animation
animato   animated
animé (F)   animated
a piacere   freely
appassionato   with passion
ardito   bold
assai   very
assez (F)   enough, rather
a tempo   return to the original tempo
    after a change
attacca   begin next section at once
aussi (F)   as

belebter (G)   lively
ben   well
bewegt (G)   moved
bien (F)   well, very
brio   vivacity, spirit, fire
brioso   with fire, spiritedly

capriccioso   capricious
calando   decreasing
calme   calm
cantabile   in a singing style
coda   end of piece
col', coll', colla, colle   with
comodo, commodo   comfortable tempo
con   with
coulé (F)   smoothly
crescendo   increasing in volume (abbr.
    cresc.)

da capo   from the beginning (abbr.
    D.C.)
dal segno   from the sign (abbr. *D.S.*)
deciso   with decision
declamato   in declamatory style
decrescendo   decreasing in volume
    (abbr. *decresc.*)
di   of, from, to
diminuendo   decreasing in volume
    (abbr. *dim.*)
dolce   soft
dolcissimo   sweetly
dolendo   doleful, sad
dolore   pain, grief
doppio   double
douce, doux (F)   soft, sweet

e   and
einfach (G)   simple, plain

energico   energetic, vigorous
ernst (G)   earnest, serious
erregeter (G)   excited
espressivo   expressive (abbr.
    espress.)
et (F)   and
etwas (G)   somewhat

feierlich (G)   solemn
ferocé (F)   wild, fierce
fine   end
flebile   tearful, plaintive
fliessende (G)   flowing
forte   loud (abbr. *f*)
forte-piano   loud, then immediately
    soft (abbr. *fp*)
fortissimo   very loud (abbr. *ff*)
forzando   with force (abbr. *fz*)
frisch (G)   glad, joyous
frölich (G)   glad, joyous
fuoco   fire

gai (F)   gay, brisk
gaiment, gayment (F)   gaily, briskly
gavotte   French dance; moderate
    tempo, quadruple time
gesangvoll (G)   in a singing style
geschwind (G)   swift, rapid
giocoso   playful
giojoso   joyful, mirthful
gioviale   jovial, cheerful
giusto   correct
gracieusement (F)   graciously
gracieux (F)   gracious
grandioso   grand, pompous
grave   slow, ponderous
grazia   grace, elegance
grazioso   graceful
gut (G)   good, well
gut zu declamiren (G)   clearly
    declaimed

heimlich (G)   mysterious
herzlich (G)   heartily, affectionate

im (G)   in
immer (G)   always
innig (G)   heartfelt, fervent
Innigkeit (G)   deep emotion
istesso   same
istesso tempo   same tempo (after a
    change of time signature)

joyeux (F)   joyous

413

klagend (G)   mourning
kurz (G)   short, crisp

Ländler   Austrian dance; slow, in
   triple time
langoureuse, langoureux
   (F)   langourous
langsam (G)   slow
langsamer (G)   slower
languido   languid
largamente   broadly
larghetto   not as slow as largo
larghissimo   very slow
largo   slow and broad, stately
lebhaft (G)   lively, animated
legato   smoothly connected
leger (F)   light
leggiero   light (abbr. *legg.*)
leicht (G)   light
leise (G)   soft
lent (F)   slow
lentement (F)   slowly
lenteur (F)   slowness
lento   slow
liberamente   freely
lieblich (G)   with charm
l'istesso tempo   same as *istesso tempo*
lustig (G)   merry, lusty

ma   but
mächtig (G)   powerful
mais sourdement agité (F)   but secretly
   agitated
maestoso,   with majesty or dignity
malinconico   in a melancholy style
marcato   marked, emphatic
marcia   march
marziale   martial
mässig (G)   moderate
même (F)   same
meno   less
mesto   sad
mezzo half   (mezzo forte, *mf*; mezzo
   piano, *mp*)
misterioso   mysteriously
mit (G)   with
moderato   moderately
modéré(F)   moderate
modérément (F)   moderately
molto   much, very
morendo   dying away
mosso   "moved" (*meno mosso,* less
   rapid; *più mosso,* more rapid)

moto   motion
munter (G)   lively, animated
mutig (G)   spirited, bold

nicht (G)   not
niente   nothing
non   not
non tanto   not so much
non troppo   not too much
nobilimente   with nobility

ossia   or
ottava   octave

parlando   singing in a speaking
   style
pas (F)   not
pastorale   pastoral
pas trop lent (F)   not too slow
pesante   heavy
peu (F)   little
peu à peu (F)   little by little
pianissimo   very soft (abbr. *pp*)
piano   soft (abbr. *p*)
più   more
plus (F)   more
poco   little
precipitando   hasty, reckless
presque (F)   almost
presto   fast, rapid
prima, primo   first

quasi   as if, nearly (as in *andante quasi
   allegretto*)

rallentando   slowing down (abbr.*rall.*)
rasch (G)   quick
religioso   religious
rêveusement lent (F)   pensively slow
rhythmique (F)   rhythmic, strongly
   accented
rigaudon   Provençal dance; moderate
   tempo, quadruple time
rinforzando   reinforcing; sudden increase in loudness for a single tone,
   chord, or passage (abbr. *rfz.*)
risoluto   strongly marked
ritardando   slowing down (abbr. *rit.*)
rubato   perform freely
ruhig (G)   quiet

sanft (G)   soft
sans (F)   without

sarabande   Spanish dance; slow tempo, triple time

scherzando   playfully

schnell (G)   fast

sec, secco   dry

segue   follows; next section follows immediately; or, continue in a similar manner

sehr (G)   very

semplice   simple

semplicemente   simply

sempre   always

sentito   with feeling

senza   without

sforzando   forcing; perform a single note or chord with sudden emphasis (abbr. *sfz.*)

siciliano   Sicilian dance; moderate tempo, $\frac{6}{8}$ or $\frac{12}{8}$ meter

simile   similarly; continue in the same manner (abbr. *sim.*)

slancio   impetuousness

sostenuto   sustained

sotto   under

sotto voce   in an undertone; subducd volume

spirito, spiritoso   spirit

staccato   detached; with distinct breaks between tones

stark (G)   strong

stendendo   slowing down (abbr. *stent.*)

stringendo   pressing onward

subito   suddenly

tant (F)   as much

tanto   so much

tempo   time

tempo giusto   correct tempo

tendrement (F)   tenderly

teneramente   tenderly

tenuto   held

tranquillo   tranquil

traurig (G)   sad

très (F)   very

triste (F)   sad

tristezza   sadness, melancholy

trop (F)   too much

troppo   too much

un, uno   one, a, an

una corda   one string; on the piano: use soft pedal (abbr. *u.c.*)

und (G)   and

unisono   unison

vif (F)   lively

vite (F)   quick

vivace   very fast

vivamente   very fast

vivo   lively

volante (F)   flowing

zart (G)   tender, delicate

zartlich (G)   tenderly

ziemlich (G)   somewhat, rather

zierlich (G)   delicate, graceful

zögerend (G)   lingering